THE ROYAL MILE

THE ROYAL MILE

EDINBURGH CASTLE TO THE
PALACE OF HOLYROODHOUSE

BY

ROBERT T. SKINNER

1947
OLIVER AND BOYD
EDINBURGH: TWEEDDALE COURT
LONDON: 98 GREAT RUSSELL STREET, W.C. 1

FIRST PUBLISHED . . . 1920
SECOND EDITION . . . 1928
THIRD EDITION, REVISED . 1947

PRINTED AND PUBLISHED IN GREAT BRITAIN
BY OLIVER AND BOYD LTD., EDINBURGH

PREFACE

No one has written—no one, it may safely be said, will ever write—a perfect account of the thoroughfare between Edinburgh Castle and the Palace of Holyroodhouse.

" The Royal Mile " is no misnomer : the distance from the inside of the drawbridge of the Castle to the entrance door of the Palace is 1 mile 106 yards.

The original drawings by Walter Geikie, R.S.A. (1795-1837), I have presented to the Edinburgh Public Library. Geikie used to sketch places in and around Edinburgh ; he was deaf and dumb, and possessed social qualities which endeared him to his brother-artists.

R. T. S.

CONTENTS

The names of places which no longer exist are in square brackets

ILLUSTRATIONS

xi

Acknowledgements are made for permission to reproduce the following Illustrations :—The Librarian, Edinburgh Public Library for the Frontispiece, VII, VIII, XXXV, XXXIX ; Paul Shillabeer for II, X, XXV and XXIX ; Francis C. Inglis for IX ; Philip Malcolm for XI ; George Waterston & Sons, Ltd., for XX, XXI, XXVI, XXXI and XXXIII ; W. J. Hay for XXIII ; *Scotsman's* Publications Ltd. for XXXVIII ; and Francis M. Chrystal for sixteen others.

THE CASTLE

Whether Edinburgh Castle was founded by a King
of the Picts or whether King Edwin of Northumbria
ever occupied it, is a moot-point; there can be no
possible doubt that King Malcolm II. (d. 1034)
made it a residence, and that here Margaret, widow
of King Malcolm Canmore, breathed her last.

The venerable pile has staged countless historic
episodes. During the rivalry of Bruce and Baliol,
the English captured the Castle, holding it for
seventeen years; Randolph, the 1st Earl of Moray,
having climbed the rock with thirty men, eventually
retook it.

Kirkaldy of Grange, doomed to be hanged at
the Mercat Cross, held the Castle from 1570 to
1573 in the interests of Queen Mary, at that time
a prisoner in England. When he surrendered to
the besieging Scots, the Regent Morton planned
and erected the Half-Moon Battery, the semicircular
platform with the one o'clock time-gun of to-day.

Another siege was that of Cromwell's Ironsides
in 1650; another that of 1689, when "Bonnie"
Dundee climbed the rock to encourage the Duke
of Gordon to continue holding the fortress for
King James VII.; a minor siege followed in 1745.

The arched pend by which the visitor ascends
the path is surmounted by the Argyll Tower.
Archibald the 9th Earl, who was imprisoned in one
of the dungeons pictured by R. L. Stevenson's *St
Ives*, spent his last night in the Tower which bears
his name and which figures in E. M. Ward's "Last
Sleep of Argyll 1685."

Forged in 1486 either at Mons or at Mollance near Castle Douglas, the old-world siege-piece, " Mons Meg," stands facing Princes Street. Associated with the Siege of Norham, the gun burst when fired in honour of the Duke of York's visit to Edinburgh in 1680 ; having found a home in the Tower of London for several years, it was brought back to Scotland in 1829.

Behind Mons Meg stands St Margaret's Chapel, the oldest place of worship in the Capital. The outer walls are of various dates. Queen Margaret seems to have built the lowermost part, her son (King David I.) completing the chancel arch.

Only recently the lower chambers and foundations of King David II.'s Tower have been discovered. Here King James III.'s brother, the Duke of Albany (1454-85), was kept prisoner ; he escaped by lowering himself from the Castle, boarding a ship at Newhaven, and fleeing to France.

On the summit of the Castle Rock stands the Scottish National War Memorial (1914-19).

Here has stood since 1760 a tank with water from Shearer Knowe, which supplies the needs of the Castle and nearly half of the Royal Mile.

The " Old Palace " contains the apartment where on June 19, 1566 Mary Stuart gave birth to the child, afterwards King James VI.

The Scottish Regalia being deposited in the Castle after the Treaty of Union (1707), Scott and others obtained Royal permission to open the chest in which they were supposed to be concealed, and there they were discovered intact (1818). The circlet worn by Bruce and arched over by King James V. figured at the coronation of King Charles II. The Sword of State was presented by Pope Julius II.

PLATE II   EDINBURGH CASTLE

See page 1

PLATE III

ST MARGARET'S CHAPEL

See page 2

to King James IV. Cardinal York, the last of the Stuarts, bequeathed the four jewels which King William IV. placed in the Castle :—(*a*) " St George," which belonged to King James VI. ; (*b*) King Charles I.'s ruby ring ; (*c*) " St Andrew," which King George VI. wears in the Palace of Holyroodhouse ; (*d*) The Collar of the Garter, presented by Queen Elizabeth to King James VI.

The Old Parliament Hall has been the scene of banquets in honour of the " Martyr " King and Oliver Cromwell. A never-to-be-forgotten feast was that of the year 1440, when the youthful Earl of Douglas and his brother were butchered in the courtyard at the instigation of Chancellor Crichton.

Castle Hill Walk (Esplanade)

The flat expanse of morainic material used to be the parade-ground for the garrison.

The order of Knight-baronet of Scotland and Nova Scotia having been instituted in 1621 by King James VI., the mandate of his successor, King Charles I., declared by a legal fiction that the soil of the Castle Hill should serve as that of Nova Scotia. The number of creations was one-hundred-and-twenty-two in King Charles I.'s reign (1625-49), no fewer than sixty-four baronets taking seisin on that historic spot.

Witches were put to death between 1479 and 1722, some on the Castle Hill Walk, the victim in most cases being strangled and the body burned thereafter.

The remains of Ensign Charles Ewart have been transferred from Salford to the north side of the Castle Esplanade ; he it was who captured a French Standard at the Battle of Waterloo.

From the Esplanade one views the Cannon Ball House : dormer window, with A. M.—M. N. 1630 (initials of the builder, Alexander Mure, skinner, and his wife, Margaret Neillems) : grooves for the shutter slides of pre-glass days, such being called " shots."

The Canon Ball may indicate the height to which water coming from the Comiston Springs can rise by gravitation.

CASTLE HILL—North Side

The street numbers are those of the Post Office Directory

Ramsay Lodge

The villa, which appears in Edgar's Plans of 1742 and 1765, and which has the octagonal tower seen from Princes Street, was built by Allan Ramsay (1686-1758), wig-maker, bookseller, and author of *The Gentle Shepherd.* The wags of the town used to speak of the villa as a goose-pie, and when Ramsay complained to Lord Elibank, his Lordship replied :— " Indeed, Allan, when I see you in it, I think they are not far wrong."

Other occupants were Mrs Grant of Laggan (1755-1838), who wrote *Letters from the Mountains* ; Sir Adam Ferguson (1771-1855), who, through the exertions of Scott, was appointed Keeper of the Regalia of Scotland ; John Galt (1779-1839), who wrote here a portion of *The Annals of the Parish* ; and George Husband Baird, D.D. (1761-1840), Principal of Edinburgh University, one of the two ministers by whom " according to the usual Scotch fashion prayers were offered up " at Abbotsford on the occasion of Scott's funeral.

An additional row of buildings was erected by Allan Ramsay the younger (1713-84), portrait-painter to King George III. Johnson, often his guest at 67 Harley Street, wrote of this artist :— " You will not find a man in whose conversation there is more instruction, more information, and more elegance."

Reservoir

Once the site of the Town's Yard which had a fire-engine station, a general depot, and a cistern for water from the Comiston Springs. The existing cistern was erected in 1851 to supply the wells of the Royal Mile. In 1681 Bruschi, a Dutchman, brought water from Comiston to the High Street. The City Records state that George Whyte, servant to Bruschi, retained the keys of the water fountains, and that a small pipe was led into the Tolbooth to supply the prisoners with water.

According to the Woodhouselee MS. of 1745 : the Highlanders " have lett owt the town sisteren in Castle hill, and the watter runs down the streats."

Ramsay Lane

The Lane is associated with Allan Ramsay (poet) and his son.

In Ramsay Lane was located the Ragged School of Thomas Guthrie, D.D. (1803-73), who conducted the institution for " city Arabs." William Watson (1796-1887), Sheriff-Substitute of Aberdeenshire, was, however, the founder in Scotland of Industrial Schools : his ashes rest at Liberton.

A Senator of the College of Justice with the title of Lord Abbotshall, Sir Andrew Ramsay was chief magistrate of Edinburgh and resided near the lane for several years. He was the first commoner styled Lord Provost, King Charles II. bestowing the honour in 1667, and giving his Lordship precedence similar to that of the Lord Mayor of London.

King James VI. had already in 1608 permitted a sword to be carried before the Provost of Edinburgh, at the same time permitting the magistrates to wear gowns.

[Bell Close]

In Bell Close, west of the Outlook Tower, stood the Cockpen mansion. Archibald Cockburn, grandfather of Lord Cockburn, purchased the estate of Cockpen in 1733 ; his widow, Martha Dundas of Arniston, styled Lady Cockpen, occupied the residence about 1761.

Outlook Tower (549)

The dormer windows having been removed, two floors were added for Short's Observatory when the Town Council persuaded the astronomer to move from Calton Hill.

Sempill's Close (541)

The Barony of Sempill dates from 1489, the original seat being at Eliotstoun in Renfrewshire, the Sempills now owning Craigievar Castle and Fintray House in Aberdeenshire.

It was a member of this house who married Mary Livingston, one of the four Marys of Mary Queen of Scots, the Queen presenting the couple with the lands of Auchtermuchty.

Francis Sempill, of Beltrees, is the reputed author of the ballad *Maggie Lauder*.

The mansion seems to have been occupied too by Grizel, sister of the 1st Earl of Rosebery and

PLATE IV

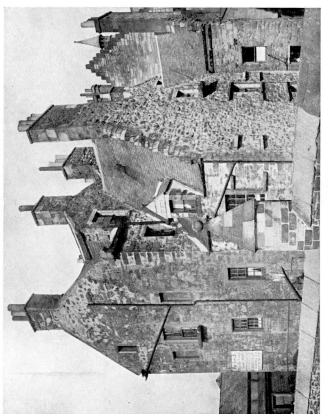

CANNON BALL HOUSE

See page 4

PLATE V

At this Postern
JOHN GRAHAM of CLAVERHOUSE
VISCOUNT DUNDEE
HELD A FINAL CONFERENCE
WITH THE DUKE of GORDON
GOVERNOR of EDINBURGH CASTLE
ON QUITTING THE CONVENTION OF ESTATES
18TH MARCH 1689.

POSTERN GATE, CASTLE

See page 8

widow of Francis, the 8th Lord Sempill, and some years later by Hugh, the 12th Lord Sempill, who was in command of the left wing of the Royal Army at Culloden (1746). This house, bearing the date 1638, which was sold in 1755 to Sir John Clerk of Penicuik, serves as kitchen for the Assembly Hall.

General Assembly Hall

Site of the so-called " palace " of Mary of Guise, mother of Mary Queen of Scots and widow of King James V. Holyroodhouse having been burned by the English under Hertford (afterwards Protector Somerset), this group of Castle Hill residences was fitted up for the Queen-Mother.

Somerset was brother-in-law to King Henry VIII. ; a descendant of his is Earl of Harewood, husband of H.R.H. Mary Princess Royal.

Formerly giving access to the " Guise Palace," certain closes (Tod's, Nairn's, Blyth's) had to be demolished to provide the site for the Hall.

In the north-west corner of Mylne's Court are seen traces of the roof and fire-places of the " Guise Palace."

The easterly portion of the Assembly Hall occupies the site of the residence of Bartholomew Somerville, who in 1640 founded the Professorship of Divinity at Edinburgh University.

The Supreme Court of the Church of Scotland meets in May, the Sovereign being represented by His Grace the Lord High Commissioner (a nobleman or a commoner). The presiding Minister, " the Right Reverend the Moderator of the General Assembly of the Church of Scotland," has precedence in Scotland for a whole year next to the Lord Chancellor of Great Britain and before the Dukes.

CASTLE HILL—South Side

Castle Wynd

A *wynd* was opened from end to end—a thorough-fare—while a *close*, being private and open at one end during the day, was closed at night.

[Blair's Close]

The children of the Castle Hill School are accommodated in the Cannon Ball House (which is of the Charles I. period, 1630), and in a new building on the site of the Gordon mansion.

George, the 1st Duke of Gordon (1643-1716), was captain and constable and keeper of the Castle (1686-89). His wife, Elizabeth Howard, daughter of the 6th Duke of Norfolk, retired to a convent in Flanders, from which she sent to the Faculty of Advocates a medal with the head of the Chevalier.

Robert Chambers asserts that Scott misrepresents fact with his *Bonnets of Bonnie Dundee*. Graham of Claverhouse (Viscount Dundee) must have led his dragoons out of the City by the Netherbow Port, and, proceeding by Leith Wynd, must have galloped along the Lang Dykes (a rough track between the George Street and the Rose Street of to-day). Clambering up the western face of the Castle Rock, Dundee held his final conference on March 18, 1689, with the Duke of Gordon either at the existing postern-gate or at a gate a few yards south : Gordon was holding the fortress for King James VII.

> The Gordon demands of him which way he goes :
> Where'er shall direct me the shade of Montrose !
> Your Grace in short space shall hear tidings of me,
> Or that low lies the bonnet of Bonnie Dundee.

PLATE VI

GORDON DOORWAY

See pages 8, 10

PLATE VII

BOSWELL'S COURT

See page 9

The mansion belonged to the Bairds of Saughton-hall early in the eighteenth century.

Mrs Cockburn, author of one version of *The Flowers of the Forest*, removed to the Gordon mansion in 1756. The name of the Close must have been changed: she wrote in 1764-65 from Baird's (not Blair's) Close to Hume, the historian, then at the British Embassy in Paris. " Not only did she divine the genius of young Walter Scott," says T. Craig-Brown, " but she gave Burns the motive for his earliest rhyme, winning both his admiration and his friendship. She knew every man and woman worth knowing in the northern capital, and with one of the greatest of men, David Hume, seems to have been on terms of intimate and familiar acquaintance."

In the same house was spent the boyhood of General Sir David Baird, Baronet (1757-1829), of Seringapatam and Corunna fame. Hearing that Hyder Ali's prisoners were chained two and two, and that young Baird was among them, the mother veiled her feelings by ejaculating—" Lord, pity the chiel that's tied to oor Davie ! "

Boswell's Court (352)

Named after Dr John Boswell, medical practitioner, uncle of Johnson's biographer. The lexicographer " spent one forenoon at my uncle Dr Boswell's, who showed him his curious museum ; and," says Boswell, " as he was an elegant scholar and a physician bred in the school of Boerhaave, Dr Johnson was pleased with his company."

The lintel reads :—

¶ O—Lord—in—The—is—al—mi—Traist.

Here in one of the flats resided Andrew Young, author of the hymn *There is a Happy Land*, which he had written at Rothesay in 1838.

One observes in the school play-ground the re-built doorway of the Duke of Gordon's residence, —over the door is a coronet supported by deer-hounds.

[Rockville Close]

Here was the residence of Alexander Gordon (1739-92), Scots judge with the title of Lord Rockville. His father was the 2nd Earl of Aberdeen ; his mother Anna, daughter of the 2nd Duke of Gordon. He was a member of the Crochallan Fencibles, the convivial club which met in Anchor Close.

[Coalstoun's or Kennedy's Close]

Chambers says that the Earl of Cassillis resided in the Close, the family name being Kennedy.

The Pre-Reformation religious house which stood here was occupied for some nineteen years by the judge, Lord Coalstoun (d. 1776). He was the Sheriff George Broun of Stevenson's *Catriona*, the defending counsel in the Appin Murder Trial.

The house of Charles Broun of Coalstoun became in 1794 the first Edinburgh Asylum for the Industrious Blind, an institution projected through the exertions of David Johnston, D.D. (1734-1824), the first Secretary. The idea originated with the blind poet, Dr Thomas Blacklock.

[Stripping Close]

Here prisoners were obliged to remove their upper garments before being whipped " at the usual

places between the Castle Hill and the Netherbow."
There were nine whipping places in the Old Town.
Three men were whipped as late as July 31, 1822.

This Close contained the printing-office of James
Donaldson (1751-1830), publisher of the *Edinburgh
Advertiser* and founder of Donaldson's Hospital, the
palatial school in West Coates opened in 1850 for
normal as well as deaf-mute children.

Tolbooth St John's Church

This edifice used first to be called the Victoria
Hall, housing till 1930 the General Assembly of the
Church of Scotland. It is an admirable specimen of
Pointed Gothic. The spire, 241 feet in height, was
designed by Agustus W. Pugin, whose name is
associated with the Houses of Parliament. The stone
was quarried from Binny, near Uphall. The architect
was James Gillespie Graham of Orchill.

The foundation-stone was laid in 1842 by
the Grand Master Mason, Lord Frederick Fitz-
Clarence, who left the Royal cavalcade for the
purpose when Queen Victoria and the Prince-
Consort were proceeding to Edinburgh Castle.

In the vestry stands the chair which the enfeebled
Knox occupied at St Giles's.

Johnston Terrace

The thoroughfare (hitherto the Western Approach
and Castle Place) was renamed after Lord Provost
Sir William Johnston (1802-88), map publisher. To
him the City owes the Meadows and the Queen's
Drive.

LAWNMARKET—North Side

The street from the West Bow to St Giles Street is known as the Lawnmarket, and a proverb runs :—" As thrang (crowded) as the Lawnmercat." The name is Land Market in Edgar's Plans of the City, 1742 and 1765, the produce of the land, even meat, having been sold here. Ainslie's Map of 1780, however, spells the name Lawnmarket.

The *Anecdotes and Egotisms* of Henry Mackenzie (1745-1831) contains the following :—

(1) " The Lawn Mercat, the chief quarter for persons of distinction. It used to be a sort of sight to go to a window there and see the ladies walking (which they always did in fair weather) along that street to the tea-parties at five in the afternoon. Dr Monro (1697-1767), one of the founders, it may be said, of the Medical School of Edinburgh, had a house there."

(2) " Stealing a room : that theft was committed by a tenant of a house in the Land Mercat, who contrived to remove a partition from the adjacent house on the same floor during the proprietor's absence in the country. I have no doubt of the fact, improbable as it is."

Mylne's Court (517)

Over the entrance is the date 1690. This " land " (a tenement with several houses) used to accommodate 54 families, but the Town Council reduced the number to 15, retaining the stone walls and restoring the interior, with two separate stairs. " Everything," writes Cockburn, " that has an old history, or an old ornament, or an old peculiarity, if it can be preserved, ought to be preserved."

Mylne's Court was the earliest attempt at city improvement, Robert Mylne (1633-1710) removing two houses to form a fashionable square. He assisted Sir William Bruce in the design for Holyroodhouse, as rebuilt under "Vice-Regent" Lauderdale. Mylne reclaimed the foreshore at Leith, and he it was who chiselled the statue of the King's goldsmith for the quadrangle of Heriot's Hospital. Robert Mylne was seventh "Master Mason to a Royal Race," the Mylnes having held that post since the reign of King James III.

A portion of the house dated 1690 was occupied by the officers of Bonnie Prince Charlie. The north-east tenements, with picturesque door, may be a century older.

James's Court (501)

The western entry, Fountainhall Close, "opposite the Bowhead well," gave access to the home of Sir John Lauder, who became a judge (Lord Fountainhall) and who acquired fame as a diarist. His first wife was the daughter of Andrew Ramsay (Lord Abbotshall).

Following Robert Mylne's example James Brownhill, wright, built this courtyard in 1725-27, modestly calling it by his own Christian name. The inhabitants of the new court were persons of no inconsiderable consequence, for they kept a clerk and a scavenger.

The north-west property, destroyed by fire, was during 1857-60 rebuilt by David Bryce, R.S.A., architect of Fettes College. One floor, third from the level of the courtyard, was the home from 1762 to 1771 of David Hume (1711-76), philosopher and

historian. When Hume went to the British Embassy
in Paris, he lent that floor to a man of letters, Hugh
Blair, D.D. (1718-1800), hence Mrs Cockburn's
allusion to Blair when writing to Hume in 1766 :—
" I am glad to hear from your sister there is no
if's of your coming to Scotland. I am glad even
that you, infidel as you are, have chased the gospel
out of James's Court." James Boswell (1740-95)
afterwards occupied the Hume floor, where he
entertained the Corsican patriot, Pascal Paoli in
September 1771. Boswell ultimately possessed the
two floors lower down and farther west, and there
he entertained Dr Johnson in August 1773, when
starting for the Hebrides. " Boswell," says one of
the lexicographer's letters, " has very handsome and
spacious rooms, level with the ground at one
side of the house, and on the other four stories
high."

The narrow windows of certain houses seem to
have given light to the closets in which the hair was
powdered.

In an upper floor lived Dr Gregory Grant, at
whose table Mrs Siddons was frequently a guest.
The musical suppers, at which Stabilini conducted,
were patronized by the Duchess of Gordon, Henry
Mackenzie, and Sir John Sinclair.

Gladstone's Land (483)

Acquired in 1631 by Thomas Gladstane, a
wealthy burgess. Near the crow-stepped gable is a
shield with his own initials and his wife's.

Here can be seen what is said to be the last
example of the City's arcading.

The masonry at the back of Gladstone's Land
used to be faced with timber. Fuel being scarce

when the City was in possession of Queen Mary in 1572, many "lands" were stripped of their timber, especially those of Her Majesty's enemies.

Lady Stair's Close (477)

The fore-stair is at least two centuries old ; no such means of access has been sanctioned by the Town Council since 1727. The hole under the fore-stair served as the shelter for the sow ! On the occasion of a Sovereign's entering the City, the fore-stair, hung with tapestry, was occupied by the rank and fashion.

Lady Stair's House bears the initials W. G. and G. S. with the date 1622. The builder was a merchant Sir William Gray (later Lord Gray) of Pittendrum, who married Gidia (Egidia or Giles) Smith, sister of Provost Sir John Smith of Groathill. Gray ruined his fortunes by his adherence to Montrose. The residence was sold about April 1719 to Elizabeth, grandchild of Lady Gray, heiress to Sir John Dundas of Newliston, and widow of John, the 1st Earl of Stair (1648-1707).

Eleanor, the 2nd Countess of Stair (formerly widow of the 1st Viscount Primrose, 1680-1706), is supposed to have been the Lady Forester of Scott's *My Aunt Margaret's Mirror*.

Agnes, mother of the 1st Lady Stair and widow of Sir John Dundas, married as her second husband Sir Archibald Primrose of Carrington (1616-79), their son Archibald becoming the 1st Earl of Rosebery.

Archibald, the 5th Earl of Rosebery, having acquired the mansion of his collateral ancestress in 1895, presented it to the City in 1907.

[Baxter's Close]

The 18th-century property of the Baxters or Bakers had to be demolished for the making of Bank Street.

Robert Burns (1759-96), coming " from the ploughtail as to an academy of gilt unbelief and artificial letters," arrived from Ayrshire on November 28, 1786. He shared a room in Baxter's Close with John Richmond, writer's clerk from Mauchline, the landlady, Mrs Carfrae, charging each 1/6 per week. " This month," says Carlyle, " he is a ruined peasant, his wages seven pounds a year, and these gone from him ; next month he is in the blaze of rank and beauty, handing down jewelled duchesses to dinner ; the cynosure of all eyes."

In Baxter's Close lived the only child of William Hamilton Nisbet of Dirleton, wife of the 7th Earl of Elgin. Whilst governess to Princess Charlotte (1796-1817), she acted as the medium of communication between the Princess and her parents (Caroline of Brunswick and the future King George IV.).

Wardrop's Court (451)

Here was the home of William Scott, the first Professor of Greek in the University, by whom the house was let to Richard Steele (1672-1729), when acting as commissioner for forfeited estates ; and here for three years lived Bain Uhyt, W.S., Founder of the Wagering Club.

Paterson's Court (441)

The proprietors in this vicinity had gardens which sloped down to the Nor' Loch. French writers of the sixteenth century knew Edinburgh as Lislebourg.

PLATE VIII

MYLNE'S COURT

See page 12

PLATE IX

GLADSTONE'S LAND

See page 14

The citizens of the Castle Hill and Lawnmarket had varied occupations, the *Edinburgh Directory* during the latter half of the eighteenth century giving the following :—money scrivener, inspector of window lights, mantua maker, clothes cleaner, gumflower maker, setter of elegant rooms, fringe manufacturer, extractor, harpsichord and spinet maker.

Bank Street

Although the structure in the Old Bank Close had its origin in 1695, yet the present Bank of Scotland, restored in 1870, was erected in 1806—the expense being defrayed from unclaimed property in the Bank's keeping.

"Three men, evidently lawyers—Walter Scott, William Erskine, William Clerk—might have been seen escaping like schoolboys from the Parliament House, and," says John Brown, " speeding arm-in-arm down Bank Street and the Mound, in the teeth of a surly blast of sleet." Erskine, afterwards Lord Kinedder, was one of Scott's companions on his voyage to the Orkneys, " the most intimate friend I had in the world "; and Clerk was the Darsie Latimer of *Redgauntlet*.

431 High Street

Here between 1816 and 1828 was a cloth-merchant's shop occupied by father and son, each named David Bridges. The junior partner is described by Lockhart (1794-1854) as an " active, intelligent, and warm-hearted fellow who has a prodigious love for the fine arts, and lives on familiar terms with all the artists of Edinburgh ; around whom in consequence of these circumstances the

C

whole connoisseurs and connoisseurship of the
north have by degrees become clustered and
concentrated, like the meeting of the red and yellow
stripes in the back of a tartan jacket."

[Galloway's Close]

"There is at Edinburgh," says the author of
Humphry Clinker, "a society or corporation of
errand-boys called caddies, who ply in the streets
at night with paper lanterns, and are very serviceable
in carrying messages. These fellows, though shabby
in their appearance and rudely familiar in their
address, are wonderfully acute, and so noted for
fidelity, that there is no instance of a caddie's having
betrayed his trust." "The moment a stranger
arrived in Edinburgh," adds Lockhart, "his face
was sure to attract the observation of some of this
indefatigable tribe, and he knew no rest till they
had ascertained his name, residence, and condition.
Whenever a stranger does arrive, it is the custom
that he enters into a kind of tacit compact with one
of the body, who is to perform all little offices he
may require during the continuance of his visit."
Colonel Mannering (according to Scott) committed
Dominie Sampson to the charge of Miles Macfin,
whom the waiter of the George Inn got at Luckie
Finlayson's in the Cowgate.

The Sheriff Court House, opened in 1937, stands
between Bank Street and St Giles Street.

[423 High Street]

Robert Seton, bookbinder, who was here in 1829,
allowed Walter Scott and Charles Kirkpatrick Sharpe
to use a window from which to witness the execution
of William Burke, who murdered men and women

PLATE X

LADY STAIR'S HOUSE

See page 15

PLATE XI

WARDROP'S COURT

See page 16

and sold their bodies to anatomists. The Burke and
Hare Murders were important in a sense, leading to
the Anatomy Act of 1832. In the roadway and
west of the stone well are three brasses which mark
the site of the gallows. On that spot was hanged in
1864 George Bryce, the Ratho murderer—the occasion
of the last public execution in Edinburgh.

[Dunbar's Close]

Here in the eighteenth century lived a glover
named Dunbar. One doubts whether Oliver Cromwell after his victory at Dunbar had a guard-house
in this Close.

St Giles Street

This street, the name of which was suggested
for the present Princes Street, is the boundary line
between the Lawnmarket and the High Street
proper.

LAWNMARKET—South Side

Free Church Assembly Hall

This Hall, throughout the year Free St Columba's
Gaelic Church, was originally St John's Free Church,
of which, Dr Thomas Guthrie, first editor of the
Sunday Magazine, was minister for about 25 years.
Gladstone and Ruskin have worshipped in St John's.

[Donaldson's Close, West Bow]

The Close led to a small court in which was the
curious edifice described by Sir Daniel Wilson :—
" It was only one storey high in addition to the
attics, on the north side, while on the south it
presented a lofty front to the Bow." Prince Charles

Edward called, during the Highland occupation of the
City, on the proprietor, Lord Provost Archibald
Stewart. The house was purchased by Alexander
Donaldson, who established the *Edinburgh Advertiser*
in 1764 and whose name is associated with the House
of Lords' decision on Literary Property (1774).
Here was born the son James Donaldson, founder
of Donaldson's Hospital (School).

West Bow

The street zigzagged down to the Grassmarket.
Sovereigns generally entered the City by the Bow :
it contained the gate built by King James II., the
" Temple Bar," so to speak, at which each received
the address of welcome. Mary Queen of Scots
came by the Bow on her return from Dunbar,
Bothwell leading her jennet ; ten days later they
were married.

John Porteous, captain of the City Guard, who
appears in *The Heart of Midlothian*, was dragged
down the Bow to his death in the Grassmarket,
September 7, 1736. " The rioters were leading or
carrying along with them the object of their ven-
geance," and when Porteous dropped one of his
slippers, " they stopped," says Scott, " sought for it,
and replaced it upon his foot with great deliberation."
Alexander Wilson, Lord Provost, having been
summoned to the House of Lords to account for
the behaviour of the citizens, was asked what kind
of shot the City Guard used at the hanging of his
namesake. The Provost answered in his native
dialect : " Such shot as in Scotland we shoot deuks
and other fools with "—" deuks " being ducks, and
" fools " fowls.

R. L. S. introduces the historic street into

Catriona :—" I was in the saddle again before the day, and the Edinburgh booths were just opening, when I clattered in by the West Bow and drew up a smoking horse at my Lord Advocate's door."

[Bow Head Corner]

From the arch of the Butter Port was lowered a " bonnie bairn " to present to Mary Queen of Scots the Keys of the City and also a Bible and a Psalm-book.

The Town Council of 1878 allowed the quaint, timber-fronted corner house to be removed, that which contained the shop in which Thomas Nelson, bookseller, 2 West Bow, began business in 1798. " I happen to have a most capricious memory," says W. E. Gladstone. " I will give you an instance. For there in the year 1826 I well remember purchasing from old Mr Nelson Isaac Barrow's *Sermons* in five volumes at the price of 26/-."

Riddle's Court (322)

Outer Portion.—The house with the corbelled door, dated 1726, was the first home of Hume after his removal from Ninewells, Berwickshire, in 1752, and here he published *Political Discourses* and began the *History of England*. " Professedly a sceptic, though by no means an atheist," says Jupiter Carlyle, " he had the greatest simplicity of mind and manners with the utmost facility and benevolence of temper of any man I ever knew.

South-west of the courtyard stood Major Weir's Land, access being had from the West Bow. A devoted member of a strict set of Covenanters and possessing the facility of *extempore* prayer, Weir made voluntary confession of certain crimes. He was burned at Gallowlee (near Shrub Place) on April 12, 1670, while the accomplice, his sister Jean, was hanged in the Grassmarket. Thomas Weir, as Major of the City Guard, had full charge of Montrose when he lay in the Tolbooth waiting execution (1650). " My rheumatism is almost gone," Scott writes in the winter of 1827, " I can walk without Major Weir, which is the name Anne gives my cane, because it is so often out of the way that it is suspected, like the staff of that famous wizard, to be capable of locomotion."

In a flat of the Outer Court was born James Pillans (1778-1864), Rector of the High School and later Professor of Humanity.

Inner Portion.—Here may be seen dormer windows, a window with the lower half a wooden shutter, gargoyles, a crane support, and a bust of Socrates.

Bailie John Macmoran, merchant, who in 1590 built the mansion, went to the High School to deal with certain boys whose conduct became unsatisfactory after they heard of a shortened vacation. They barred themselves into the class-rooms, and, when trying to force the door, Macmoran was shot dead by William Sinclair (1595). Eight of the boys were confined for a few days in the Tolbooth.

Here at " Macmoran's Lodging " in 1598 the City banqueted King James VI., his Queen (Anne of Denmark), with her brother, the Duke of Holstein. The hall with its quaint panels is well worth a visit.

In this Court lived Sir John Smith of Groathill, the Edinburgh Provost of 1643, one of the commissioners who proceeded to Breda to assure King Charles II. of General Monk's loyalty.

PLATE XII

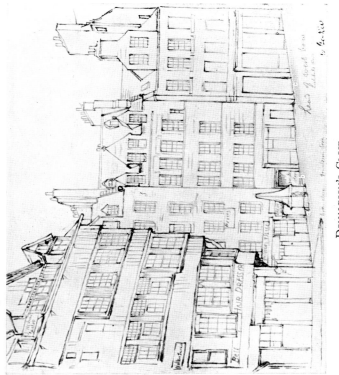

DONALDSON'S CLOSE

See page 19

Plate XIII

Lord Provost Stewart's Residence

See page 20

Lord Advocate Prestongrange lived for a time in Riddle's Close, and there, according to Stevenson's *Catriona*, he discussed with David Balfour of Shaws who the Appin murderer really was, Balfour telling his Lordship that he had but the one design, " to see justice executed and the innocent go clear."

Fisher's Close (312)

The town residence of the Buccleuchs.

Henry the 3rd Duke (1746-1812), travelling abroad with his brother Hew, had as tutor Adam Smith, author of *The Wealth of Nations*. In Paris Smith met Hume, Voltaire, le Sage, and Turgot.

Brodie's Close (304)

The Close once extended from the Lawnmarket to the Cowgate.

Roman Eagle Hall was the meeting place of the Lodge Roman Eagle, No. 160, whose charter was granted on February 7, 1785 and whose first Master was Dr John Brown, founder of the Brownonian System of Medicine. For some years the members, principally medical men, wrote their records in Latin. The plaster ceiling is dated 1645 and 1646.

William Brodie, Town Councillor and Deacon of the Wrights, lived at the lower end of the Close— " well seen in good society, crafty with his hands as a cabinet-maker, and one who could sing a song with taste " (R. L. S.). W. E. Henley and Stevenson collaborated in *The Double Life* :—" On with the new coat and into the new life. Down with the deacon, and up with the robber ! There's something in hypocrisy after all. If we were as good as we seem, what would the world be ? " Breaking into the

General Excise Office in Chessels Court, Brodie
abstracted a few pounds. Arrested at Amsterdam,
he was tried in Edinburgh before four judges ;
Braxfield (" Weir of Hermiston ") presided, the jury
including Burns's Edinburgh publisher (William
Creech) and the Founders of Donaldson's Hospital
and Fettes College. Brodie and his accomplice,
George Smith, grocer, were hanged at the Tolbooth
on October 1, 1788. A confederate of Brodie's,
John Brown, perhaps the biggest rogue of the party,
turned King's evidence at the trial. Brodie bribed
the executioner to allow him to wear a steel collar
to prevent strangulation, and, after being hanged,
Brodie was wheeled rapidly along the street—all to
no purpose !

Buchanan's Court (300)

The uppermost window of the spiral staircase
affords a panoramic vista ; the buildings from
Riddle's Close to Buchanan's Court date from the
reign of King Charles I.

Buchanan's Land is reputed to occupy the site
of the residence of the Abbot of Cambuskenneth.

William Wastle of *Peter's Letters* had in the
Lawnmarket " a very snug house, although by no
means in a fashionable part of the town. From a
feeling of respect for his ancestors, he refuses to
quit the old family residence, which is no other than
a lodging up five pair of stairs, in one of those huge
aerial edifices of the Old Town—edifices which
sometimes contain beneath a single roof a population,
layer above layer, household above household, more
numerous than that of many a street in many a city
south of the ideal line."

PLATE XIV

BRODIE'S CLOSE

See page 23

PLATE XV

OLD BANK CLOSE (Gourlay House on left)

See page 25

[Old Bank Close]

Practically in a line with the west pavement of Melbourne Place, contained the residence of Robert Gourlay, messenger-at-arms at Holyroodhouse, and a favourite with King James VI.

To Gourlay's " Lodging," then occupied by the English Commander at the siege of the Castle in 1573, were conducted Kirkaldy, Maitland of Lethington, and others who had surrendered.

Here the ex-Regent Morton spent the last days of his life, and in his conferences with the clergy protested his innocence of Darnley's murder. He was beheaded with the Maiden in 1581. " 'Tis an axe, man, an axe, which falls of itself like a sash window, and never gives the headsman the trouble to wield it " (*The Abbot*).

King James VI. himself resided in the Gourlay house 1593-94.

At the upper end of Old Bank Close Lord President Sir George Lockhart was shot by a disappointed litigant, John Chiesley of Dalry, in 1689. The murderer was hanged with the pistol round his neck. Says Scott in *The Bride of Lammermoor* :—" The fate of Chiesley was a sufficient warning to any one who should dare to assume the office of avenger of his own imaginary wrongs."

In this Close was founded the Bank of Scotland (1695).

[Libberton's Wynd]

Johnnie Dowie's Tavern, not infrequently patronised by the poets Fergusson and Burns, was demolished in 1834. Dowie figures in Kay's *Portraits*.

From each stone well standing in the High

D

Street—known in the North of England as the
" pant "—water was carried to the lofty compounds
by male and female porters.

> There, from the earth the labouring porters bear
> The elements of fire and water high in air.

Buccleuch Statue

Walter, the 5th Duke of Buccleuch (1806-84),
when a lad of sixteen, entertained King George IV.
for a fortnight at Dalkeith House. Scott wrote of
him four years later :—" If God and the world spare
him, he will be far known as a true Scots lord."
The statue is by Sir Edgar Boehm, while the pedestal
with scenes from the history of the Clan Scott—each
the work of an Edinburgh sculptor—was designed by
Sir Rowand Anderson.

[Tolbooth Prison]

At the north-west corner of St Giles's Church
stood the Tolbooth, " Heart of Midlothian." Paving
stones mark the boundaries of the Prison, the " heart "
denoting approximately the position of the door.
" This was the site of the Tolbooth, the Heart of
Midlothian, a place old in story and name—father
to a noble book " (R. L. Stevenson).

The Prison, erected on or before 1561, was sold
for upwards of two hundred pounds, and swept away
in 1817 on the erection of a more suitable place on
the Calton Hill. The " high and antique building
with turrets and iron grates " was the meeting-
place of the Scots Parliament, serving in succession
as Town Hall, as chambers for the Privy Council,
as College of Justice, and after 1640 as jail for debtors
and criminals, " A living grave. But yet I wish the
building had been spared. It was of great age ; it

was incorporated with much curious history ; and
its outside was picturesque " (Cockburn). To the
north gable were affixed pikes for the heads of
distinguished victims of the law. The rebels of
the first Jacobite Rising were confined in the
Tolbooth. In the condemned cell of the Tolbooth
lay the unhappy Effie Deans of Scott's *Heart of
Midlothian*. " Many a poor devil dangled like a
tassel at the west end of it, while the hawkers were
shouting a confession the culprit had never heard
of " (Scott).

The annex of two storeys projected westwards,
its roof forming the scaffold for criminals, such as
Deacon Brodie.

[Luckenbooths]

In the High Street stood the Luckenbooths
(*i.e.* locked booths), removed in 1817. The passage
between the west Luckenbooths and the houses on
the north side of the High Street was some fifteen
feet wide. " This would be undoubtedly one of the
noblest streets in Europe, if an ugly mass of mean
buildings, called the Luckenbooths, had not thrust
itself, by what accident I know not, into the middle of
the way, like Middle-Row in Holborn " (Smollett).

The first floor of the eastern Luckenbooths was
occupied by Allan Ramsay in 1726 ; here as bookseller he set up the first circulating library in
Scotland. In front of the shop were displayed
models of the heads of Ben Jonson and Drummond
of Hawthornden, familiar to the citizens as " The
Twa Heids." Gay, of *Beggar's Opera* fame, when
in Edinburgh with the Duke and the Duchess of
Queensberry in 1732, the last year of his life, enjoyed
sitting at Ramsay's windows. Smollett, who des-

cribes Edinburgh as " a hot-bed of genius," pictures
in *Humphry Clinker* the scene when " all the people
of business at Edinburgh, and even the genteel
company, may be seen standing in crowds every
day, from one to two in the afternoon, in the open
street."

Ramsay's premises sixty years later were used by
the booksellers, Alexander Kincaid and William
Creech, each in turn Lord Provost of the City.
Creech (1745-1815), who published for Burns the
Edinburgh Edition of the *Poems*, was one of the
founders of the Speculative Society in 1764, a select
body with which Walter Scott and R. L. Stevenson
were actively connected. The position of Creech's
shop " in the very tideway of all our business," says
Cockburn, "made it the natural resort of lawyers,
authors, and all sorts of literary idlers, who were
always buzzing about the convenient hive."

[Krames]

The passage between the Luckenbooths and
St Giles's was called locally the Creams. " Shopless
traffickers first began to nestle there about the year
1550 or 1560, and their successors stuck to the spot
till 1817, when they were all swept away." " In my
boyhood," says Cockburn, " their little stands, each
enclosed in a tiny room of its own, and during the
day all open to the little footpath that ran between
the two rows of them, and all glittering with attractions, contained everything fascinating to childhood,
but chiefly toys. It was like one of the Arabian
Nights bazaars in Bagdad. Throughout the whole
year it was an enchantment. Let anyone fancy what
it was about the New Year, when every child had
got its handsel, and every farthing of every handsel

was spent there. The Krames was the paradise of childhood."

" In one of those little shops plastered like so many swallows' nests among the buttresses of the old Cathedral, that familiar autocrat, King James VI., would gladly share a bottle of wine with George Heriot the Goldsmith " (R. L. Stevenson).

ST GILES'S

High Kirk (St Giles's)

A church was founded by King Alexander I. in 1120 on the site where a place of worship had stood since 854. St Giles's, " the premier church to-day in world Presbyterianism," was consecrated by David de Bernam, Bishop of St Andrews, on October 6, 1243. King Richard II. is said to have " committed to the flames the noble town of Edinburgh, with the Church of St Giles " (1385). The date is important, for two years later the Town Council began to enlarge the Church by adding five chapels on the south of the nave (from the west gable to the south transept) ; and from this date nearly until the Reformation the Church increased in length, breadth, and height ; for example, the capitals of the pillars in the nave were at one time seven courses lower than those now existing. The Cathedral, stands by the side of the highway, like all other churches dedicated to St Giles. Some years after the Reformation there were three divisions—the High, the Old, and the Tolbooth Church ; a fourth being formed in 1689—the New Church or " Haddo's Hole "—where Sir John Gordon of Haddo, a Royalist member of the Aberdeen family, was imprisoned till beheaded in 1644. Founding the bishopric of Edinburgh in 1633—Edinburgh had until now been in the diocese of St Andrews—King Charles I. made St Giles's his Cathedral, ordering the partitions to be removed from end to end : the first Bishop was William Forbes. Some thirty years previous to the Revolution of 1690 the partitions seem to have been replaced. A Church of England clergyman, James Brome by name, travelling in Scotland, mentions that in 1669 the Cathedral was in six portions. The Church, as Johnson observed in 1773, had lost its original magnificence " by being divided into four places of presbyterian worship." " ' Come,' said Johnson jocularly to Principal Robertson, ' let me see what was once a church.' We entered that division which was formerly called the New Church, and of late the High Church, so well known by the eloquence of Dr Hugh Blair " (Boswell). The Cathedral was unfortunately given over to the " tender mercies " of William Burn, architect, whose hands it left in 1834 a brave kirk, of well-jointed mason work, no longer possessing what Andrew Fairservice, thinking of Glasgow Cathedral, calls " curlie-wurlies and open-steek hems " (*Rob Roy*).

Between 1872 and 1883 St Giles's was restored to much of its pristine grandeur by William Chambers, LL.D. (1800-83), publisher, a former Lord Provost, the church being reopened on May 20, 1883. Chambers had accepted the offer of a baronetcy made to him by Gladstone, and the baronetcy would have been announced on the anniversary of the birth of Queen Victoria, May 24, had Chambers not died four days before.

In the south transept was buried Lord James Stewart, Earl of Moray, " a good and godly governor," assassinated at Linlithgow in 1570. Knox preached the funeral sermon.

On Sunday, July 23, 1637, a riot was caused by the attempted introduction of the King Charles I. service-book. The tradition is that during the fracas a woman threw her stool at Dean Hanna with the words :—" Will ye say mass at my lug ? "

The Crown Tower of St Giles's was built in 1648. Under this Tower rested the body of Earl Haig (February 4 to 7, 1928).

The remains of James Graham, the 1st Marquess of Montrose (1612-50), " the stainless Cavalier," were laid in the Chepman Aisle eleven years after his execution, while in 1888 a monument was erected over the grave at the instigation of Queen Victoria.

Criminals under sentence of death attended service in the Tolbooth Church (the south-west portion of the Cathedral) every Sunday previous to execution. When the congregation had all but assembled one Sunday morning in 1736, Andrew Wilson, smuggler, seized two of the guard, fastening his teeth in the collar of a third, thus enabling George Robertson, a companion in misfortune, to escape. John Porteous, Captain of the City Guard, was on duty at Wilson's execution in the Grassmarket ; when a disturbance arose, his men opened fire, killing some spectators and wounding others. As the result of this, Porteous was sentenced to death. Queen Caroline granted a respite for six weeks, at the end of which period King George II. would be home from the Continent. The postponement led to the Porteous Riots. When Alexander Carlyle, D.D., Jupiter Carlyle of Inveresk (1722-1805), was a boy, he was taken by an acquaintance to church to see Wilson and Robertson, and later, from a window in the Grassmarket, Carlyle saw the execution of Wilson.

The paved court to the south of St Giles's was a garden until 1477 when the Provost of the Church converted it into a graveyard extending down to the Cowgate. The letters I. K. and the date 1572 are supposed to have indicated at onetime the last resting-place of Knox. " He sleeps within call of the church that so often echoed to his preaching," (R. L. Stevenson). " Here lies one who never feared the face of man," observed the Regent Morton, standing bare-headed at the grave of the Reformer. When Parliament Square was being altered, the remains of many citizens must have been carted to Greyfriars Churchyard.

After John Knox the best-known ministers are Alexander Henderson (1583-1646), a keen opponent of " Laud's Liturgy " and a promoter of the National League and Covenant ; Principal William Carstares (1649-1715), the most influential personage in Britain during the reign of King William III. ; Hugh Blair (1718-1800). " I love Blair's sermons," said Dr Johnson. " Though the dog is a Scotsman and a Presbyterian, and everything he should not be, I was the first to praise them ! " Johnson wished Blair to " come over to the Church of England."

In unveiling the Memorial to R. L. S. in the Moray Aisle in 1904, Archibald, Lord Rosebery said :—" Is it not a pathetic thought that this Scottish genius, so pre-eminently Scottish, should have laid his bones, not in the Lothians that he loved so well, or even in the land which he adorned with his genius, but in the far distant islands of the Pacific ? "

In the Parliament Close—Cockburn's " most

Plate XVI

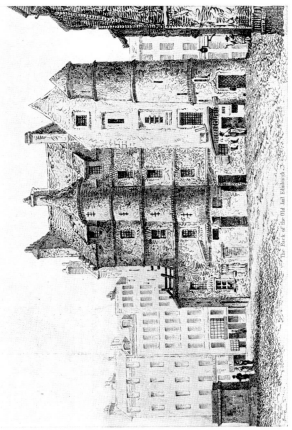

"The Back of the Old Jail Edinburgh."

Tolbooth, "Heart of Midlothian"

See page 26

PLATE XVII

ST GILES'S TOWER

See page 31

continental-looking spot in Edinburgh "—was situated the print-shop of John Kay (1742-1826), early in life a barber and later a miniature-painter and caricaturist, whose portrait sketches—Kay's *Portraits*—furnish a picture of the Edinburgh of those days.

All the shops seem to have been removed in September 1818.

The equestrian statue of King Charles II. stands in Parliament Square (formerly Close). After the fire of November 1824 the figure was removed for safety to the Calton Jail, where it lay for eleven years.

On the west and south sides of the Cathedral stood the booths of booksellers, furriers, watch-makers, goldsmiths; one booth, only seven feet square, belonged to George Heriot (1563-1624), who bequeathed his fortune to found a residential school for boys. Heriot advanced sums of money to King James VI. and the Queen, and so important a personage did he become that an apartment was assigned to him in Holyroodhouse. Heriot is the " Jingling Geordie " of *The Fortunes of Nigel*.

Another booth was that of Peter Williamson (1730-99), from Aboyne, who published the first *Edinburgh Directory* (1773) and established a penny post.

Parliament House stands on the site of the manses of the City ministers.

HIGH STREET—North Side

Regia Via are the words used in old writs for the King's highway.

" I descended lower to the City wherein I observed

E

the fairest, the goodliest streete that ever mine eyes beheld, for I did never see or heare of a streete of that length " (John Taylor, 1580-1653, the Water-Poet).

" The principal street of Edinburgh was then, as now, one of the most spacious in Europe," writes Scott in *The Abbot*. " The extreme height of the houses, and the variety of Gothic gables, and battlements, and balconies, by which the sky-line on each side was crowned and terminated, together with the width of the street itself, might have struck with surprise a more practised eye than that of young Graeme."

Byers Close (373)

On the left resided John Byers, merchant, a " truly good and excellent citizen," who about 1610 purchased the estate of Coittes (Coates), where St Mary's Cathedral now stands. Becoming City Treasurer, Bailie, Dean of Guild, and the so-called " Old Provost," he died in 1629 aged 60. His son, Sir John Byers, erected East Coates House.

Down the Close on the right is the house of Adam Bothwell (d. 1593), Bishop of Orkney, Lord of Session, and Commendator of Holyrood, who " after the protestant form " married Mary Stuart to James Hepburn, Lord Bothwell (May 15, 1567), Darnley having been murdered so recently as February 10. The same Bishop Bothwell crowned Queen Mary's son at Stirling five days after her abdication. The sister of Bishop Bothwell became the mother of John Napier, inventor of logarithms.

The hexagonal apse (best seen from Advocate's Close) has Latin mottoes over the dormer windows :— Exitus acta probat (Ovid) (The end justifies the deeds) : Nihil est ex omni parte beatum (Horace)

PLATE XVIII

BISHOP BOTHWELL'S HOUSE

See page 34

PLATE XIX

ADVOCATE'S CLOSE

See page 36

(There is no such thing in the world as unmixed happiness).

In the High Street between Byers Close and the Advocate's stood the abode of Sir William Dick of Braid (d. 1655). Dick was one of those who lent money to King James VI., and, while Provost of Edinburgh, he financed the Covenanters (1638-39).

In *The Heart of Midlothian* Scott represents David Deans as saying that his father saw men " toom the sacks of dollars out o' Provost Dick's window *intill* the carts that carried them to the army at Dunse Law." Dick advanced £20,000 for the cause of King Charles II., the Parliamentary party ultimately fining him £65,000. Reduced to indigence, he proceeded to London in the hope of recovering £160,000, which he had lent on government security. He was more than once imprisoned for petty debts, and, when he died in his lodgings at Westminster, his means were such as to deny him a decent burial.

The judge Coalstoun, when residing in Byers Close, happened one morning to lean out of his window, gowned and wigged. Two tomboys of the upper floor were suspending a kitten by means of a string. The tradition is that the kitten seized his Lordship's wig !

Sir William Dick's house was subsequently occupied by the 1st Earl of Kintore, hence the Cantore's or Kintyre's Close of early Directories. The Regalia of Scotland having been removed by Mrs Grainger from Dunnottar to Kinneff, the mother of Kintore circulated a report that her son had carried the Regalia abroad.

Advocate's Close (357)

The Close takes its name from Sir James Steuart of Goodtrees, whose residence was demolished in 1882. Twice Lord Advocate (1692-1709 and 1711-13), he witnessed the Restoration, the Revolution, and the Union.

In Advocate's Close two centuries later resided Andrew Crosbie, advocate (d. 1785), one of the two characters whom Scott pictured as Counsellor Pleydell in *Guy Mannering*. " On entering the house, Mannering was struck with the narrowness and meanness of the wainscotted passage. But the library into which he was shown by an elderly, respectable-looking man-servant, was a simple contrast to these unpromising appearances " ; and Mannering was delighted " with the view from the windows which commanded that incomparable prospect of the ground between Edinburgh and the sea— the Firth of Forth, with its islands."

When Johnson visited Edinburgh in 1773, Andrew Crosbie was the only man who, in Lord Stowell's opinion, " was disposed to stand up to Johnson." This eminent advocate forsook Advocate's Close for a mansion on the east side of St Andrew Square, which became Douglas's Hotel and in which Scott spent the last two nights in his own romantic town.

A door in the Close is inscribed C. C.—H. B. 1590—Clement Cor and Helen Bellenden.

Roxburgh's Close (343)

Here in the reign of King James VI. lived a cook named John Roxburgh.

The Close has no connection whatever with the ducal family of Roxburghe.

[Wariston Close]

John Murdo, shoemaker, was here in 1586.

The buildings in this stretch of the High Street used until recently to have arcaded fronts.

Here stood the house occupied by John Knox, " an old Hebrew prophet in the guise of an Edinburgh minister of the sixteenth century." Here in 1560 his first wife, Marjorie Bowes, died, and here in 1564 he had as companion the second wife Margaret Stewart.

In this Close resided Archibald Johnston (1611-63), who resisted King Charles I. in an attempt to force the English ritual upon the Kirk, and who was one of the framers of the National Covenant to oppose whatever tended towards prelacy. Among concessions to the Covenanters, the King three years later made Johnston a lord of session, when he took the courtesy title of Lord Wariston (1641). Eventually a member of the Cromwell House of Peers, he was singled out at the Restoration and hanged at the Mercat Cross (1663). King Charles II.'s desire for the execution of this " canny, lynx-eyed lawyer and austere presbyterian zealot " was such that Lauderdale protested against delay.

[Writers' Court]

Long ago a notice-board hung here—" Writers' Court," the Writers to the Signet, a prominent legal body, having found a home for their Library in 1699.

Chrystal Croftangry, imaginary editor of *Chronicles of the Canongate*, a young barrister with no fees, " laughed and made others laugh, and drank claret at Walker's," an old tavern in Writers' Court.

Another haunt was " The Star and Garter," kept by one Clerihugh, and there Colonel Mannering and Dandie Dinmont saw Pleydell and his frolicsome company in " high jinks " *Guy Mannering*, Chapter XXXVI.

In this vicinity lived Alexander Nasmyth (1758-1840), portrait and landscape painter. Robert Burns was the artist's most distinguished sitter. They used to walk together to Arthurs Seat.

Royal Exchange

Erected in 1753-61 and enlarged in 1901, this building, intended for the use of merchants who had hitherto transacted business in Parliament Close, became the City Chambers, *i.e.* Town Hall. The Royal Exchange marked the first instalment of an Improvement Scheme initiated by Lord Provost George Drummond (1687-1766). Drummond used to tell his friends that he was not the projector of the Scheme—he was only executing what the unfortunate King James VII. proposed as Duke of York.

In the Court in front of the City Chambers stands Sir John Steell's group of Alexander and Bucephalus.

" Within the Exchange " lived for some years Alexander Wood (1725-1807), the surgeon who was consulted regarding Scott's lameness. It was " Lang Sandy Wood " who attended Burns in St James's Square after an accident to his knee and who got him a post under the Commissioners of Excise.

[Allan's Close]

Here Deacon Brodie concealed his skeleton keys, crowbars, and other unlawful tools.

PLATE XX

Craig's Close July 1853

CRAIG'S CLOSE

See page 39

PLATE XXI

OLD POST OFFICE CLOSE

See page 40

[Craig's Close]

The lintel of the principal doorway used to be inscribed 1744.

In Craig's Close stood the printing house of Andrew Hart (d. 1621), who brought out an edition of the Bible (1610); while in the same Close James Watson printed his *Choice Collection of Comic and Serious Scottish Poems*, the medium by which Burns became acquainted with the older poets.

In the Close resided Burns's Edinburgh publisher, William Creech (1745-1815), and later, Scott's publisher, Archibald Constable (1774-1827).

During Creech's absence in London in 1787, Burns addressed him in the humorous poem, *Willie's Awa*.

Here Archibald Constable is believed to have resided in 1795. The opening chapters of *Waverley* having been shown to Constable in 1814, he detected the authorship, and arranged afterwards to publish the novel and to divide the profits with the Author. The firms of Constable and Ballantyne becoming insolvent, Scott found himself involved to the extent of £120,000. " Poor Mr Pole, the harper, sent to offer me £500 or £600, probably his all," writes Scott. " There is much good in the world, after all. But I will involve no friend, either rich or poor. My own right hand shall do it." In 1827 Scott spoke of Constable as " a prince of booksellers ; his views sharp, powerful, and liberal ; too sanguine, however, and like many bold and successful schemers, never knowing when to stand or stop, and not always calculating his means to his objects with mercantile accuracy." In the *Chronicles of the Canongate*, written after the commercial catastrophe, the romancer wrote of himself :—" I bought, and built, and planted, and was considered by myself as by the rest of the world, in the safe possession of an easy fortune. My riches, however, like the other riches of this world, were liable to accidents, under which they were ultimately destined to take unto themselves wings and fly away. The year 1825, so disastrous to many branches of industry and commerce, did not spare the market of literature ; and the sudden ruin that fell on so many of the booksellers could scarcely have been expected to leave unscathed one whose career had of necessity connected him deeply and extensively with the pecuniary transactions of that profession." From a window of Constable's house Scott and the youthful Prince Gustavus, son of the ex-King of Sweden, witnessed the proclamation of King George IV. at the Mercat Cross. " On that occasion," according to Lockhart, " the air of sadness that mixed in the Prince's features with eager curiosity, was very affecting."

The *Edinburgh Review* being founded in 1802 by Sydney Smith, Jeffrey, Horner, and Brougham, the confederates used to meet secretly in " a dingy room off Willison's printing-office at Craig's Close," Willison having been the father-in-law of Constable.

[Old Post Office Close]

The Post Office, which was here in the reign of King George I., was moved to a stair on the south side of Parliament Close, one letter-carrier sufficing for the needs of the City. The Post Office seems later to have been housed behind the Law Courts in a building once occupied by Lockhart of Covington. The Post Office was afterwards " the northmost house on the west side of the North Bridge " ; it stood later on the Regent Bridge ; finally the Crown erected the present G.P.O.

At Matthew Thomson's Tavern in the Old Post Office Close, the Wagering Club, held its first annual meeting. It was founded in 1775 by Bain Whyt, W.S., " whose happy flow of humour, moral worth, and genuine kindness endeared him to all his friends."

Anchor Close (243)

This Close contained the town house of Lord Provost George Drummond, first Master of the Merchant Company (1681). During the sixth and last period of his provostship the Nor' Loch was drained.

In the Close William Smellie (1740-95), printer, naturalist, antiquary, printed the first edition of *The Encyclopædia Britannica* (three volumes). The firm, Creech and Smellie, produced the Edinburgh edition of Burns's *Poems*, 1787. The poet himself read the proofs on the premises. Smellie introduced Burns to the Crochallan Club, which met in a tavern in Anchor Close. The Club got its name from a Gaelic song which the landlord, Daniel Douglas, sang to his customers ; the members included Hon. Henry Erskine, Lord Newton, and Lord Rockville.

Geddes Entry (233)

Geddes seems to have been a surgeon. The Cape Club sometimes held its meetings in Walter Scott's Tavern in this entry. In the course of his inauguration each member had to kiss a large poker

F

reverently, and take his designation from some scrape
in which he had been involved.

No. 231.—" Opposite the guard " stood (and
still stands) the shop of James Gillespie (1726-97),
founder of Gillespie's Hospital, who manufactured
snuff at Spylaw, Colinton.

" Above Gillespie's Shop " died in 1826 John
Kay, caricaturist, whose own shop was then in
Parliament Close.

North Foulis Close (229)

The town house, perhaps, of Munro of Foulis
(Ross-shire), Colonel Sir Hector Munro being
created a baronet of Nova Scotia in 1634.

Sir Harry Munro, the 7th baronet, was uncle to
Henry Mackenzie, " The Man of Feeling."

Old Stamp Office Close (221)

Here until 1821 was situated the Stamp Office,
and here from 1727 to 1753 was the Royal Bank.

In the Close resided for some years Susanna,
(1689-1780), third wife of the 9th Earl of Eglintoun,
mother of the 10th and 11th Earls, the personage to
whom Allan Ramsay dedicated *The Gentle Shepherd*,
" in a fulsome style of panegyric," and to whom he
presented the original manuscript. " She was of the
noble house of Kennedy," says Boswell, " and had
all the elevation which the consciousness of such
birth inspires. Her figure was majestic, her manners
high-bred, her reading extensive, and her conversation elegant. She had been the admiration of the
gay circles of life, and the patroness of poets." The
Countess received Johnson at Auchans in Ayrshire

on his return from the Hebrides in 1773. Then in her eighty-fifth year, and married the year before he was born, she told him " that she might have been his mother and that she now adopted him." " When we were going away," says Boswell, " she embraced him, saying, ' My dear son, farewell '." The Countess and her seven daughters were noted for gracefulness of feature—" the Eglintoun air." One of Edinburgh's attractions was seeing them leave each by sedan chair for the Assembly Rooms.

The Eglintoun residence became between 1750 and 1787 a fashionable tavern, John Fortune's ; it existed until about 1796. The Lord High Commissioner to the General Assembly held levees in Fortune's, thence proceeding to St Giles's, even ladies in court dress walking in the procession. The Earl of Hopetoun entertained here while Lord High Commissioner in 1754.

In this Close (according to some Highlanders) Flora Macdonald (1722-90) finished her education at Miss Henderson's boarding-school, Flora having been sent to Edinburgh via Glasgow by Lady Margaret MacDonald of Monkstadt, Skye.

The Poker Club, instituted in 1762, moved after some years to Fortune's, the members including Adam Ferguson, David Hume, Hugh Blair, Joseph Black, and Adam Smith.

It was at Fortune's that the Wig Club originally met in 1775. Chambers says the Wigs usually drank the old Scottish ale called Two-penny, with which " they ate souters' clods, a coarse, lumpish kind of loaf."

Scott and Jeffrey, it may be remembered, one day " rushed from George Square " to sup at Fortune's.

Jackson's Close (209)

The houses in this vicinity are of old date.

William Nicol (1744-97), classical scholar, whom Walter Scott, his pupil, condemned as " worthless, drunken, and inhumanly cruel to the boys under his charge," left the High School to open an academy in Jackson's Land " for instructing young gentlemen in the Latin language." Nicol accompanied Burns during a three weeks' tour in the Highlands, starting on August 25, 1787 ; Burns had spent the previous eighteen days with this " obstinate son of Latin prose " in a flat over Buccleuch Pend.

Milne Square

Benjamin Franklin, arriving in Edinburgh, went to Mrs Cowan's boarding-house (September 3, 1759).

Fleshmarket Close (199)

After her surrender at Carberry Hill, Queen Mary was lodged " fornent the croce, upon the north syd of the gait " in the house belonging to David Makgill, but rented by Sir Simon Preston, of Preston and Craigmillar, Provost of Edinburgh. Formerly one of the Queen's trusted friends, Preston supported the Lords after her marriage with Bothwell. Historians favour the view that Sir Simon, accordingly, conducted Queen Mary to his " loging " in the vicinity of Fleshmarket Close, such being known as the Black Turnpyke.

Here resided David Aikenhead, Provost four times in the seventeenth century, the Close being sometimes called " The Provost's."

Deacon William Brodie, frequented a gambling-house in the Close.

The third floor was occupied by Henry Dundas,

Lord Melville (1742-1811), when he first practised as advocate.

Paterson's, later Cameron's, Tavern was the meeting-place of the Marrow-Bone Club, whose members were all Whigs and whose motto was " Nil nisi bonum." They used to meet until 1873.

Cockburn Street

The thoroughfare is named out of compliment to the judge, Lord Cockburn (1779-1854).

The cellar of the National Bank in the High Street was at one time the dingy tavern, the Union Cellar, where some of the signatures were obtained for the Treaty of Union (1707).

[177 High Street]

From the cellar " opposite the Tron Kirk," that is, from the laigh shop of W. Bell at 177 High Street, the coach described by Scott in *The Antiquary* started for *the* Queen's Ferry.

" The lady of the subterranean mansion " was then Mrs Macleuchar, " a sharp-looking dame, with a pair of spectacles on a very thin nose, who inhabited a ' *laigh* shop ' (that is, an area) opening to the High Street by a strait and steep stair, at the bottom of which she sold tape, thread, needles, skeans of worsted, coarse linen cloth, and such feminine gear."

[Cap and Feather Close]

Swept away for the North Bridge. Here was born Robert Fergusson (1750-74), whom Burns styled " my elder brother in misfortune, by far my elder brother in the muses." Son of Aberdeen-shire parents, he was hailed at twenty-one as the successor of Alan Ramsay. A fall down some steps necessitated his removal to a primitive asylum near Bristo Port, where he died.

North Bridge

The present structure dates from 1900. The foundation stone of the first bridge across the valley was laid in 1763 by " that noble-minded citizen of Edinburgh," Lord Provost Drummond, but when nearly completed in 1769, a portion of the bridge fell, burying some persons in the ruins. The site of the bridge was formerly the bed of the Nor' Loch. The Bridge was opened in 1772. When the Fish Market was removed to a place under the North Bridge, " there was an outcry as if hereditary nastiness, like other abuses, had been made by time necessary for comfort " (Cockburn).

Carrubers Close (135)

Opposite this stands the old well, in a line with which stood the forestair leading to the premises of Allan Ramsay at " The Sign of the Mercury." The register recording the baptism of his children styles him a " piriwige " maker in 1713, a " weegmaker " in 1714, and a bookseller in 1725. Ramsay removed in 1722 to the site between Borthwick's Close and the Old Assembly Close, and from there he issued *The Ever Green* (a collection of Scots Poems) and the *Gentle Shepherd*. Leigh Hunt regarded Ramsay " in some respects the best pastoral writer in the world." In Carrubers Close Ramsay built " at vast expense " a theatre, for which the magistrates, influenced by the clergy, refused to grant a licence.

In this Close resided John Spottiswood (1565-1639), Archbishop of St Andrews and Scots historian. King Charles I. wished him to have precedence

before the Lord Chancellor of Scotland, but, on the
death of Kinnoull in 1635, Spottiswood himself
became Chancellor. He it was who crowned King
Charles I. at Holyroodhouse in 1633, being assisted
by bishops " in white rochets and sleeves, and copes
of gold having blue silk to their feet," a ceremonial
which estranged the King's Scottish subjects.

At the house of Samuel Mitchelson, Writer to
the Signet, Matthew Bramble dined on " singed
sheep's head and haggis." " The first," says
Smollett, " put me in mind of the history of Congo,
in which I read of negroes' heads sold publicly in
the markets. The last, being a mess of minced
lights, livers, suet, oat-meal, onions, and pepper,
enclosed in a sheep's stomach, had a very sudden
effect on mine, and the delicate Mrs Tabby changed
colour."

Henry Mackenzie regarded Mitchelson as an
uncommonly good performer on the German flute.

One of Mitchelson's apprentices was Robert
Ainslie, W.S. (1766-1838), who in 1787 rode with
Robert Burns into Teviotdale and Berwickshire.

Bishop's Close (129)

The original residence appears to have been built
by Thomas Saintserf or Sydeserf (1581-1663),
successively Bishop of Brechin, Galloway, and
Orkney. His friendship with Archbishop Laud made
him a mark for the violence of the Presbyterians.

Henry Dundas, Lord Melville, was born at
Bishop's Land in 1742. The Melville column, in
St Andrew Square, was wont to remind the Ettrick
Shepherd of " some giant condemned to perpetual
imprisonment on his pedestal, and mournin' ower
the desolation of the city that in life he loved so

well, unheeded and unhonoured for a season in the great metropolitan heart o' the country which he aince rejoiced to enrich and beautify, telling and teaching her how to hold up her head bauldly among the nations " (*Noctes Ambrosianae*).

Among the residenters of the " land " in 1752 was Lady Jane Douglas Stewart (1698-1753), the talented daughter of the 2nd Marquess of Douglas. In 1746 Lady Jane was married at Drumsheugh House to Colonel (afterwards Sir John) Stewart of Grandtully, two years later giving birth to twins at Paris. She was then fifty years of age. In 1752 she returned from Paris to Edinburgh. In April 1753 the younger twin died, the mother seven months later. In 1754 Lady Jane's brother, Duke of Douglas (1694-1761), settled his huge estates on the Hamiltons, but in six years he revoked the settlement in favour of his surviving nephew. The Court of Session, sitting in Holyroodhouse, decided for the ducal house of Hamilton by eight votes to seven, the House of Lords reversing the judgment two years later.

In 1790 Archibald Stewart was created Lord Douglas of Douglas, a title now extinct.

In Bishop's Land during the winter of 1786-87 Burns got three lessons in French every week at 9 p.m. from Louis Cauvin, junior (1754-1825), son of the founder of Cauvin's Hospital for Boys. Cauvin senior is said to have been a footman in the family of Lady Jane Douglas, and may have come from France as a witness in the Douglas Lawsuit.

North Gray's Close (125)

Down in Jeffrey Street stands the Episcopal Chapel built after the congregation were expelled from St Giles's in 1689. It became the religious centre of the Jacobite party in the City. Here have worshipped Thomas Ruddiman, Baroness Nairne, ballad-writer, and William Edmonstoune Aytoun, poet. To Sir William Forbes of Pitsligo, banker, is owing the credit of giving Scottish episcopalians " a real and sure standing " in Edinburgh.

Morrison's Close (117)

The vaulted ground-floor of a house here served as the oratory of a religious body.

John Ruskin's grandfather moved to this Close from Kennedy's.

Bailie Fyfe's Close (107)

Gilbert Fyfe was the senior bailie of Edinburgh in 1686. Here Francis Jeffrey (1773-1850), editor of the *Edinburgh Review*, and afterwards Scots judge, attended John Cockburn's school; at eight he was transferred to the High School.

Nathaniel Gow (1766-1831), son of Niel Gow, resided in Bailie Fyfe's Close when a young man; as a teacher of the violin and pianoforte he commanded the highest fees, and sometimes played at the private parties given by King George IV.

Paisley Close (101)

The High Street shop on the right of the opening was that of Lord Provost Sir William Fettes, Bart. (1750-1836), founder of Fettes College. A wine and tea merchant, he was also a contractor for military stores.

G

Chalmers Close (81)

Here stood the town house of the Hopes, ancestors of the Marquess of Linlithgow.

At the lower end of the Close stands Trinity College Church. At the back has been re-erected a small portion of the Church founded in 1462 by King James II.'s Queen, Mary of Gueldres, and removed to make way for a siding at the Waverley Station. It was one of the finest examples in Scotland of a church of that period ; the high windows were specially fine.

On the morning of Sunday, November 24, 1861, Nos. 99 to 103 High Street, " ran together with a hideous uproar and tumbled story upon story to the ground," no fewer than thirty-five persons being killed. When the rescuers were at work, a boy (Joseph M'Ivor), pinned down by the debris, was heard shouting : " Heave awa', lads, I'm no deid yet." The keystone of the modern arch bears the boy's head. The civil engineers who reported on the accident, ascribed it " to the removal of the large portion of the central wall on the shop floor."

Monteith's Close (61)

Here lived James Kennedy (d. 1465), grandson of King Robert III., and counsellor to King James II. and King James III. Bishop of Dunkeld and afterwards of St Andrews, he founded St Salvator's College, endowing it with the teinds of four parishes which till then had belonged to the bishopric.

In 1835 died at the age of 106 Widow Grant, who, beginning at 3 a.m., used to carry water from the well to flats.

PLATE XXII

ALLAN RAMSAY'S SHOP AND HOUSE (ON LEFT)

See page 46

PLATE XXIII

JOHN KNOX HOUSE

See page 51

Trunk Close (55)

" Trunk " may be a corruption of " Turing " (pronounced *Tierwin*, locally *Torn*), the Turings being baronets of Foveran in Aberdeenshire. The Close provides a notable specimen of Scottish domestic architecture.

A bill for repealing the statutes against Roman Catholics having been introduced in 1779, some rioters burned a house in Trunk Close supposed to be a chapel, but in reality the residence of the Popish Bishop.

Near the Close is the public well which used to stand at the mouth of Fountain Close.

Moubray House (53)

Daniel Defoe (1661-1731), author of *Robinson Crusoe*, became editor of the *Edinburgh Courant* in 1710 :—" Edinburgh, printed by John Moncur, for the undertakers, and to be sold at Mr John Johnston's house, almost at the foot of Moubray's Close, at the Netherbow."

Moubray House, a tavern in the eighteenth century, boasted a room with panelled walls and decorated ceiling. It was once the bookshop of Archibald Constable, and here was born James Drummond, R.S.A. (1816-77), whose historic pictures are well known.

John Knox House (45)

The letters J. M. are the initials of James Mosman, Goldsmith to Mary Queen of Scots ; M. A. those of Mariot Arres, his wife. The figure pointing to the sun emerging from clouds is apparently Moses.

The picturesque edifice with projecting angle was occupied for three months by the Reformer John

Knox, the owner of the place having taken refuge in the Castle. When the Castle was garrisoned by Kirkaldy of Grange, in the cause of Queen Mary, and when Kirkaldy accused John Knox of slander, the Churchman quitted Edinburgh for St Andrews (May 1571). He returned to Edinburgh in August 1572 to die. James Mosman was serving with Kirkaldy, and it is possible that the magistrates may have placed Knox in the house vacated by the jeweller Mosman. On November 9, Knox preached in St Giles's at the ordination of a colleague, James Lawson. He never left his home again, dying on November 24. " Have you hope ? they asked Knox in his last moments. Unable to speak, he lifted his finger, pointed upwards, and so died. Honour to him ! His works have not died. The letter of his work dies, as of all men's ; but the spirit of it never " (Carlyle, *Heroes and Hero-Worship*). No entry appears in the Town Council Minutes to guide the citizens as to where Knox lived during the last months of his life—August 23 to November 24.

Moray-Knox Church

This Church occupies the site of the Balmerino mansion.

From Lord John the Town Council acquired the superiority of the lands of Calton (or Caldtoun) in 1724. Lord Arthur, staunch Jacobite and last member of the family, was beheaded on Tower Hill in 1746.

Within the railings of the Church have been deposited a few of the stones from the Netherbow. " The heads of the preachers were frequently exposed on pikes between their two hands, the

palms displayed as in the attitude of prayer." Here
Lord Wariston's head was exposed with that of his
friend, James Guthrie, minister of Stirling, com-
memorated by the inscription on the Martyrs'
Monument at Greyfriars. The boy Guthrie figures
in *The Lays of the Kirk and Covenant* by Mrs A.
Stuart Menteath :—

> Oh ! a strange, sad sight was the converse mute
> Of the dead and the living there ;
> And thoughts in that young child's soul took root,
> Which manhood might scarcely bear !
>
> But ever he meekly went his way,
> As the stars came o'er the place—
> And his mother wept, as she heard him say,
> " I have seen my father's face ! "

Netherbow

One of the principal ports or gates of the City,
" bow " meaning " arch." The original Netherbow
suffered considerably during the Hertford invasion
of 1544.

The second Netherbow with tower and spire was
demolished in 1764. The clock and weather-vane are
now at the Orphan Hospital.

" The Netherbow Port might be called the
Temple Bar of Edinburgh : intersecting the High
Street at its termination, it divided Edinburgh,
properly so called, from the suburb named the
Canongate, as Temple Bar separates London from
Westminster " (*Heart of Midlothian*).

Prince Charles Edward's followers met with no
opposition while entering the Capital by the Netherbow. " Just as the Highlanders reached the gate,"
writes Chambers, " it was opened by the guard

within, in order to let out the hackney coach which
had brought back the deputies from Slateford. The
coach was returning to the Ramsay stables in the
Cowgate. No sooner did the portal open than the
Highlanders rushed in and took possession of the
gate."

HIGH STREET—South Side

Mercat Cross

The structure, from which the Lyon King of
Arms makes Royal Proclamations, was erected in
1885 by the Right Honourable William Ewart
Gladstone (1809-98), who claimed " a purely Scottish
descent," and who was Member of Parliament for
Midlothian from 1880 to 1895. The shaft used to
be the central feature of the original Cross. The
first Cross, which stood near the north-east corner
of St Giles's, was moved farther east in 1617. From
the Mercat Cross came the " awful summons "
dissuading King James IV. from war with England :—

> Then on its battlements they saw
> A vision, passing Nature's law,
> Strange, wild, and dimly seen ;
> Figures that seemed to rise and die,
> Gibber and sigh, advance and fly.
>
> *Marmion.*

[New Bank Close]

Down the Close stood, until 1820, the New Bank
or Royal Bank, whose stock at the formation of the
Company in 1727 exceeded that of the Bank of
Scotland.

At the upper end of the Close stood the shop
of Alexander Donaldson, bookseller, who figured in

PLATE XXIV

A View of the *NETHERBOW PORT* of EDINBURGH from the West
This ancient Fabric was taken down 31ʳᵈ of August 76↓.

NETHERBOW PORT

See page 53

PLATE XXV

MERCAT CROSS

See pages 54, 55

the House of Lords Copyright Case of 1774; he was succeeded here by his son, James Donaldson, founder of Donaldson's Hospital.

Upstairs (with a door from the New Bank Close) was the writing-school of William Swanson, " the great hand-spoiler of the time " : thus he is described by Lord Cockburn, one of his pupils. Even in boyhood the budding judge interested himself in the shop of Creech hard by :—" I always tried to get a seat next a window, that I might see the men I heard so much talked of moving into and out of this bower of the muses, or loitering about its entrance."

In Salamander Land was presented to the public Patrick O'Brien, Irishman, eight feet one inch in height.

Site of Mercat Cross

Near the mouth of the Old Fishmarket Close are outlined in the street the paved foundations of the Mercat Cross erected there in 1617. Scott carted to Abbotsford " the very fountain that in days of yore graced the Cross of Edinburgh, and flowed with claret at the coronation of the Stuarts." Scott lamented the barbarity of the " Auld Reekie bailies " in removing the Gothic Cross, to widen the thoroughfare :—

> Dun-Edin's Cross, a pillared stone,
> Rose on a turret octagon
> (But now is razed that monument,
> Whence royal edict rang,
> And voice of Scotland's law was sent
> In glorious trumpet-clang.
> Oh, be his tomb as lead to lead,
> Upon its dull destroyer's head !
> A ministrel's malison is said).

At the Mercat Cross perished Kirkaldy of Grange (1573), for the "keeping of the Castle against the King and his Regent." On the site farther east perished Huntly (1649); Montrose (1650), "his booke and declaratione tayed in a rope aboute his necke"; James Guthrie (1661); Wariston (1663); the Argylls (1661 and 1685). Kirkaldy and Montrose were hanged.

King James VI. appeared at the Cross on the twenty-first anniversary of his birth, anxious to reconcile his nobles by making the contentious parties walk through the City hand in hand; on that day he released all persons imprisoned for debt.

Writing of the crossing of Queen Anne from Denmark in 1589, an old chronicler says that "the tempest of storme, bayth be sea and land, was sae vehement that many ships pereshit upoun the sea, sae that the passage for Queyne Anne was veri difficult to cum in Scotland." The wizard, Richie Graham, tried for the raising of the storms, was convicted and burned at the Mercat Cross.

Prince Charles Edward being established in Edinburgh in 1745, the followers proclaimed his father at the Cross. David Beatt, a Jacobite teacher, read the commission of regency, "with the declaration dated at Rome 1743, and a manifesto in the name of Charles, Prince Regent, dated at Paris May 16, 1745. Mrs Murray of Broughton, whose enthusiasm was surpassed only by her beauty, sat on horseback at the Cross, a drawn sword in her hand, her person profusely decorated with the white ribbons which signified devotion to the House of Stuart" (Chambers, *Rebellion in Scotland*). In 1746 Charles Edward's banners, captured at Culloden, were burned at the Cross by order of Cumberland;

the banners were carried in procession from the Castle by the hangman and thirteen chimney-sweepers.

The Mercat Cross, an encumbrance to the street, was removed in 1756, and preserved at the Drum, Midlothian until 1869.

Old Fishmarket Close (190)

At the lower end until the dawn of the nineteenth century was held the fishmarket described by Cockburn as " a steep, narrow, stinking ravine." " The fish," says he, " were generally thrown out in the street at the head of the Close, whence they were dragged down by dirty boys or dirtier women ; and then sold unwashed—for there was not a drop of water in the place—from old, rickety, scaly, wooden tables, exposed to all the rain, dust and filth." Poultry the women disposed of later.

In the Close until a few years ago might have been seen the dwelling of the hangman or doomster. The last whose name is recorded, John High, died in 1817. The hangman was also called " the lad in the *piot* (*i.e.* magpie) coat," his livery of black or dark gray being ornamented with silver lace.

George Heriot, founder of Heriot's Hospital, took up house in Fishmarket Close, while, according to tradition, Defoe worked in the Close, being secret agent for the English Government at the Union.

Borthwick's Close (186)

The Close took its name from the family of Lord Borthwick, the Barony dating back to 1452.

On November 15, 1824 a number of tenements between St Giles's and the Tron, with others in the

north-eastern corner of the Parliament Close, went
on fire ; " before morning a range of houses six
or seven stories high, with fifteen windows in front
and extending back almost to Cowgate—as dense a
mass of buildings as was perhaps in the world—
was a burnt shell " (Cockburn). The only building
in the High Street which escaped destruction—
" Salamander Land "—contained the shop of James
Donaldson, founder of Donaldson's Hospital ; it
was pulled down in 1847 for the extension of the
Police Office.

Old Assembly Close (172)

In this Close, opposite which stands a well,
resided Sir Alexander Gibson (Lord President
Durie), who died in 1644. He was kidnapped by a
suitor, Lord Traquair, who regarded him as un-
favourable in a cause before the court, and who
kept him for two or three months in a dark room
in the Tower of Graham, Annandale (Scott, *Christie's
Will*).

" The Assembly," a private association for
dancing, was formed in 1710, the headquarters
being a " land " in the West Bow. The next rooms,
however, were in the Old Assembly Close, 1720-56.
Oliver Goldsmith (1728-74), medical student, visited
" The Assembly " in 1753, finding " one end of the
room taken up by the ladies who sat dismally in a
group by themselves. On the other end stand their
pensive partners that are to be, but no more inter-
course between the sexes than between two countries
at war." Though the Scots were never congenial
to Goldsmith's taste, yet he frankly recognised the
beauty of the women and the good breeding of the
men.

In the Old Assembly Close at the printing premises of Kirkwood & Sons, originated the Great Fire of 1824.

Covenant Close (162)

The National Covenant being approved in Greyfriars Church, one of the copies lay for signature at a house in Covenant Close (1638).

In the Close resided for a time Robert Macqueen, Lord Braxfield (1722-99), "Weir of Hermiston." "God was love; the name of my lord (to all who knew him) was fear" (R. L. Stevenson). "The giant of the Bench was Braxfield," writes Cockburn; "his very name makes people start yet. Strong built and dark, with rough eyebrows, powerful eyes, threatening lips, and a low growling voice, he was like a formidable blacksmith. His language, like his thoughts, was short, strong, and conclusive."

"Betimes in the morning, having taken our breakfast, we got a caddie to guide us and our wallise to Widow McVicar's, at the head of the Covenanters' Close. Mrs McVicar kept a cloth shop, and sold plaidings and flannels, besides Yorkshire superfines, and was used to the sudden incoming of strangers, especially visitants from both the West and the North Highlands" (Galt, *Annals of the Parish*).

When "Chrystal Croftangry" was, like other young lairds, "sweeping the boards of the Parliament House with the skirts of his gown," he used occasionally to "eat oysters in the Covenant Close" (*Chronicles of the Canongate*).

Nanty Ewart's father sent him at "nineteen to study divinity at the head of the highest stair in the Covenant Close" (*Redgauntlet*).

Burnet's Close (156)

Here lived Samuel Burnet, a brewer, and here stood the town house of Lord Auchinleck, Scots judge (1706-82), father of James Boswell, the biographer of Johnson. At Auchinleck (pronounced Affleck) Johnson " came in collision " with the judge, who used afterwards to speak of him as " Ursa Major."

[Guard House]

In the middle of the street the City Guard had their headquarters, " a long, low, ugly building (removed in 1787), which to a fanciful imagination might have suggested the idea of a long black snail crawling up the middle of the High Street, and deforming its beautiful esplanade " (*Heart of Midlothian*). In front of the building was placed " the wooden mare," on which a veteran might have been seen mounted, " a firelock tied to each foot, atoning for some small offence."

Clam Shell House (150)

Here Mary Stuart seems to have taken shelter on her return from Dunbar with Darnley—Riccio had been murdered recently in the Palace of Holyroodhouse.

Bell's Wynd (146)

The third Edinburgh Assembly Rooms were opened in this Wynd in 1756. Hugo Arnot states that " the profits were given for the support of the Charity Workhouse. Minuets were danced by each set, previous to the country dances. Strict regularity with respect to dress and decorum, and great dignity of manners were observed," says Alan Fairford in

Redgauntlet. "They begin to talk of a new Assembly Room." "A new Assembly Room," exclaimed the old Jacobite laird. "Umph,—I mind quartering three hundred men in the Old Assembly Room."

The fourth Edinburgh Assembly Rooms—the present handsome apartments in George Street—were opened in 1787 ; there at the Theatrical Fund Dinner on February 23, 1827 Lord Meadowbank divulged, with Scott's consent, the identity of the Great Unknown, Sir Walter corroborating with the remark that he was the " total and undivided author " of the Waverley Novels.

Stevenlaw's Close (132)

This name is taken from Steven Loch or Law, a supporter of Queen Mary during the Civil War of 1571.

In the Close was the Roman Catholic Chapel in which Prince Charles Edward worshipped.

The *City Directory* of 1784 has a curious entry, "Mrs Fraser, pastry mistress, Stevenlaw's Close."

In 1786-87 Burns used to call on Allan Masterton in Stevenlaw's Close. Masterton was later the High School writing-master, the Allan of the song—

> O Willie brewed a peck o' maut,
> And Rob and Allan cam' to pree.

The air is Masterton's, the song Burns's. William Nicol, another High School master, had Burns and Masterton as guests at Moffat one autumn ; the trio had so joyous a time that they agreed thus " to celebrate the business." Burns spoke of Masterton as " one of the worthiest men in the world, and a man of real genius."

[Kennedy's Close]

Here died George Buchanan (1506-82), who resigned the Principalship of St Andrews University in order to tutor Prince James (afterwards King James VI.), then in his fourth year, and who, Johnson considers, " has as fair a claim to immortality as can be conferred by modern Latinity." Buchanan maintained that the Casket Letters were in Queen Mary's handwriting.

The " Crown " in Kennedy's Close was one of the haunts of the Knights of the Cape Club. The members included Alexander Runciman (painter) ; David Herd (literary adviser to Constable) ; Henry Raeburn (*Sir Discovery*) ; and Robert Fergusson (*Sir Precentor*).

In this Close stood the premises of John Ruskin's grandfather, calico merchant.

Tron Kirk

Here stood the " tron," a public beam for weighing goods.

The Tron Kirk, a good example of " Laudian Gothic," was founded in 1637 by order of King Charles I. to house a congregation displaced from St Giles's when the royal charter of September 29, 1633 made the great church serve as the cathedral. A notable feature of the Tron interior is the oaken roof. The church plate is of great beauty, two of the communion cups being inscribed 1633.

William Erskine, a seventeenth-century cleric, exclaimed during prayer :—" Lord, have mercy on all fools and idiots, particularly on the magistrates of Edinburgh ! ''

Among the seat-holders in the eighteenth century were Lord Provost Drummond and Professor Adam Ferguson, together with judges such as Elchies, Nisbet, Methven, Tinwald, Gardenstone, Braxfield, Hailes, Monboddo, and Strichen.

Dr Thomas Chalmers was Moderator of the General Assembly which met in the Tron Kirk in 1832.

The day after the great fire of November 15, 1824 '' an alarm was given that the Tron Church was on fire. We ran out from the Court, gowned and wigged,'' writes Cockburn, '' and saw that it was the steeple, an old Dutch thing, composed of wood, iron, and lead, and edged all the way up with bits of ornament. When it was all over, and we were beginning to move back to our clients, Scott, whose father's pew had been in the Tron Church, lingered a moment, and said, with a profound heave, ' Eh, sirs ! mony a weary, weary sermon hae I heard beneath that steeple ' ! ''

When Colonel Mannering reached the High Street, it was '' clanging with the voices of oyster-women and the bells of pye-men ; for it had, as his guide assured him, just ' chappit eight upon the Tron.' ''

Edinburgh was a disorderly town in the sixteenth and seventeenth centuries. '' George of Seyton,'' says Norton to Murray in *The Abbot*, '' was crossing the causeway this morning with a score of men at his back, and had a ruffle with my friends of the house of Leslie ; they met at the Tron, and were fighting hard, when the provost with his guard of partizans came in thirdsman, and staved them asunder with their halberds, as men part dog and bear."

South Bridge

Sir William Forbes of Pitsligo (1739-1806), the banker whom Pitt was wont to consult, shares with his partner Lord Provost Sir James Hunter Blair (1741-87) the credit of building the South Bridge, twenty-two arches opening up communication with the southern suburbs. The Bridge was finished in 1788. As a boy of eight, Henry Cockburn was conducted to the High School daily by his tutor. " The only thing that relieved my alarm as he hauled me along," says Cockburn, " was the diversion of crossing on planks the arches of the South Bridge which were then unfinished."

At the point where the High Street and the Bridges intersect was buried (at his own request) Walter Merlion, French mason, who in the time of King James V. paved the footpaths of the chief street of the City.

Niddry Street

Francis Earl of Bothwell (d. 1624) persecuted King James VI. and his Queen, and here in 1591 Provost Nicoll Edward gave shelter to the Royal couple. Bothwell had consulted two witches about the King's end, James VI. regarding the Earl with dread ever after.

St Cecilia's Hall, once the home of classical concert, was built in 1762 by Robert Mylne after the model of the Opera House at Parma ; the same Mylne was architect of the Blackfriars Bridge over the Thames. It was said of Mylne that his private houses never smoked !

PLATE XXVI

MORTON'S RESIDENCE

See page 67

Henry Mackenzie's *Anecdotes and Egotisms* cannot be quoted too often. " Some of the houses had a double entry from Niddry's and Merlin's Wynds. I remember a mistake of a lady's chair man carrying her, first to a wrong door in the one wynd, when she was ushered into a drawing-room. Her mistake, being discovered, she made her apology and returned to her chair, the bearers of which were directed to the house she wished to go to, of which the proper door was in the other wynd. She was carried thither accordingly, but unluckily to the other entry of the very house she had left, and on being admitted was ushered into the self-same drawing-room."

Wedding the words to a melody popular at the time, Andrew Young (1807-89), Head Master of Bell's School, No. 30 Niddry Street, wrote the hymn *There is a Happy Land*. It was written while he was on holiday in Rothesay.

[Dickson's Close]

Here resided David Allan, R.S.A. (1744-96), who illustrated Ramsay and Burns.

Cant's Close (70)

This Close is named from the family of Cant, owners of Priestfield and the Grange of St Giles. The properties adjoining the Close once belonged to the Church of Crichton in Midlothian.

" There is such bandying of private feuds and public factions that a man of any note shall not cross your High Street twice without endangering his life thrice " (*Fortunes of Nigel*). Sir Walter Scott of Buccleuch was murdered in 1552 by the

I

Kerrs of Cessford, a family with which the old feud continued.

> When the streets of high Dunedin
> Saw lances gleam, and falchions redden,
> And heard the slogan's deadly yell—
> Then the chief of Branksome fell.
> *Lay of the Last Minstrel.*

Strichen's Close (66)

The Close derives its name from the Judge of Session, Alexander Fraser, Lord Strichen (d. 1775), who occupied the former lodging of the Abbot of Melrose. He married Anne, daughter of the 1st Duke of Argyll. From Lord Strichen and his wife is descended the present Lord Lovat.

Here resided Walter Chepman (d. 1538), the first printer in Scotland. He served the City as Dean of Guild. He was buried in the aisle built by himself on the south side of St Giles's Cathedral.

This Close contained the mansion of Sir George Mackenzie of Rosehaugh, " Bloody " Mackenzie, King's Advocate, who prosecuted the Covenanters.

Blackfriars Street

The Monastery of the Black Friars, founded in 1230 by King Alexander II., stood in the Cowgate.

The Wynd of this name was the scene of the brawl—" Cleanse the Causeway " (1520)—between the adherents of the Earl of Arran (d. 1529), whose grandfather was King James II., and those of the Earl of Angus (d. 1557), whose wife, Margaret, was widow of King James IV. The parties, " each headed by a person of importance, chanced to meet in the very centre of the street, or, as it was called, in ' the crown of the causeway '—a post of honour

as tenaciously asserted in Scotland as that of giving
or taking the wall used to be in the more southern
part of the island. The two leaders being of equal
rank, and most probably, either animated by political
dislike or by recollection of some feudal enmity,
marched close up to each other, without yielding an
inch to the right or the left ; and neither showing
the least purpose of giving way, they stopped for an
instant, and then drew their swords. Their followers
imitated their example " (*The Abbot*).

The mansion at the lower end of Blackfriars
Street (east side) was occupied by James Beaton
(d. 1539), Archbishop of Glasgow and St Andrews,
and by his more celebrated nephew, Cardinal David
Beaton (1494-1546).

Walter Chepman and Andrew Myllar set up a
printing press in the Cowgate near the Beaton
mansion, from which in 1508 they issued the first
book printed in Scotland.

After the interview with Darnley at the Kirk o'
Field on February 9, 1567, Queen Mary passed along
Blackfriars Wynd on the way to the Palace of
Holyroodhouse, while the conspirators carrying gun-
powder made their way down Todrick's Wynd, an
alley farther east.

Blackfriars Street's only remaining antiquity is
the residence, with a coat of arms over the entrance,
of James the 4th Earl of Morton, who, having been
implicated in Darnley's murder, perished by the
Maiden in 1581. This beheading machine was used
in Scotland from 1565 down to 1710. " Earl Morton
hath brought you down a Maiden from Halifax, you
never saw the like of her," says Michael Wing-the-
Wind in *The Abbot*, " and she'll clasp you round the
neck, and your head will remain in her arms." A

scutcheon over a door in the New Town " somewhat jars in sentiment where there is a washing at every window " (R. L. Stevenson).

During his visit to Edinburgh in 1773, Johnson worshipped in the chapel founded by Lord Chief Baron Smith for the service of the Church of England, the Rev. George Carr (1704-76) preaching from the words :—" The Lord reigneth, let the earth rejoice." Boswell was " sorry to think Mr Johnson did not attend to the sermon, Mr Carr's low voice not being strong enough to reach his hearing."

South Gray's Close (40)

The tablet on the High Street frontage records the birth of the 11th Earl of Buchan's sons—the Hon. Henry Erskine (1746-1817), orator, wit, Dean of Faculty and Lord Advocate, and the Hon. Thomas Erskine (1750-1823), afterwards Lord Chancellor of Great Britain and Baron Erskine of Restormel. Henry Erskine was the best-natured man Scott ever knew, thoroughly a gentleman.

In the Close is seen a portion of the City Wall of 1472, generally called The Flodden Wall.

The mansion of Lord Elphinstone stood lower down the Close until 1927, and opposite it, until sixty years ago, the Scottish Mint. There was a certain Lady Elphinstone who reached the age of 103, and who, a keen Whig, did not relish Graham of Claverhouse. The great soldier is said to have visited her in order to hear her describe some scenes of which she had been a witness. " Indeed," said she, " I think one of the most remarkable is, that when I entered the world there was one Knox deaving us a' with his clavers, and now that I am going out of it, there is one Clavers deaving us with his knocks." The Elphinstone property passed to Peter Wedderburn of Chesterhall, elevated to the bench as Lord Chesterhall, and in the house was born his eldest son, Alexander Wedderburn (1733-1805), who rose to be Lord Chancellor Loughborough, the 1st Earl of Rosslyn.

What is now St Patrick's Roman Catholic Church was opened in 1774 as a place of worship for Episcopalians. The ceiling over the altar was painted by Alexander Runciman. One of the clergy was Archibald Alison (1757-1839), whose wife was the sister of Dr James Gregory, compounder of Gregory's Mixture. Alison wrote essays on *Taste* ; his only defect, thought Cockburn, was " the odd one of too much politeness." Maria Edgeworth went to hear Alison :—" His fine voice but little altered. To me he appears the best preacher I have ever heard." " No man ever wrote a better sermon," said Dugald Stewart, " no man ever spoke a better sermon, no man ever thought a better sermon."

Hyndford Close (34)

The name is taken from the family of Hyndford, the title becoming extinct in 1817. John Carmichael, the 3rd Earl (1701-67), was envoy to three European Courts.

On the west side of the Close lived the mother of Lady Anne Barnard (1750-1825), who wrote *Auld Robin Gray*, taking the name of the ballad from the old herd at Balcarres. In *The Pirate* Scott compared the condition of Minna Troil, " Queen of the Swords," with that of Jeanie Gray, the village heroine in Lady Anne Barnard's ballad.

In the same house lived Jean Maxwell, daughter of Sir William Maxwell of Monreith, and wife of

Alexander, the 4th Duke of Gordon (1743-1827). Her beauty may be judged from the portrait by Sir Joshua Reynolds. She was the sole arbitress of fashion in Edinburgh. Three of her daughters married Dukes (Richmond, Manchester, Bedford), another a Marquess (Cornwallis), another a Baronet. She entertained Burns with other literati during the winter of 1786-87. Charles Kirkpatrick Sharpe says of her :—" I never saw a vulgar duchess except the Duchess of Gordon." Scott's opinion being that her " sole claim to wit rested upon her brazen impudence and disregard to the feelings of all who were near her." For some years the Duchess was estranged from her husband, leading a wandering life, and dying in poor circumstances at a Piccadilly hotel on April 11, 1812.

A house, once the property of the Earls of Selkirk, was occupied later by Dr Daniel Rutherford (1749-1819), physician and botanist, half-brother of Scott's mother.

North of this stood Lodge St David at which Scott was made a Freemason on March 2, 1801.

Fountain Close (22)

The fountain or public well on the other side of the High Street used to stand at the mouth of this Close, hence the name. The Town Council permitted the Incorporated Trades of Calton to lay a pipe for water from the fountain well.

In this Close Thomas Bassendyne (d. 1577) printed the earliest translation of the New Testament published in Scotland, having already brought out an edition of the works of Sir David Lindsay.

Here Oliver & Boyd, the publishing firm founded in 1778, occupied towards the end of the eighteenth century a portion of the Hall of the Royal College of Physicians.

Tweeddale Court (14)

The spelling of the name in old Directories is Tweddle or Twedles. The mansion with its gates of wrought iron was built by Dame Margaret Kerr, daughter of the 1st Earl of Lothian, wife of the 7th Lord Hay of Yester, and founder of Lady Yester's Church. The shelter for sedan chairs remains. The gardens, famed for their lime trees, extended down to the pillared entrance gate in the Cowgate.

The Tweeddale mansion became the Head Office of the British Linen Bank. One dark evening in 1806 a porter, William Begbie, was carrying a parcel of bank notes from the Leith Branch, when a scoundrel stabbed him to the heart in Tweeddale Court, and carried off £4392. The murderer was never discovered. At the Theatrical Club Dinner in the George Street Assembly Rooms in 1827, Lord Meadowbank revealed the parentage of the Waverley Novels. " Shortly after resuming his chair," says Lockhart, " Sir Walter (I am told) sent a slip of paper to Mr Patrick Robertson, begging him to confess something too,—why not the murder of Begbie ? "

The Governors of the British Linen Bank were succeeded in 1817 by Oliver & Boyd, publishers.

World's End Close (10)

Here stood the residence of Sir James Stanfield, of Newmills, East Lothian, whose murder in 1687 was a mystery connected with the politics of the time of King James VII. The belief that the body of the person murdered bleeds at the touch of the murderer was urged as evidence of guilt at the trial of the son, Philip Stanfield.

> Young Stanfield touch'd his father's corpse,
>   When rose a fearful wail ;
> For blood gush'd from the winding-sheet,
>   And every face grew pale.
>
> JAMES MILLER.

Says Scott :—" I see nothing inconsistent with the old gentleman's having committed suicide. The ordeal of touching the corpse was observed in Germany. They call it *barrecht*."

In the World's End Close was born William Falconer (1732-69), the adventurous spirit whose poem, *The Shipwreck*, was founded upon his own experiences as a sailor.

CANONGATE—NORTH SIDE

The word Canongate has no connection with " gate." " Canongate " = canon—gait, the latter meaning " way." Compare Bishopsgate, Gallowgate, Highgate. The canons who walked along this " way " towards Edinburgh were the monks of Holyrood Abbey—Canons Regular of the Order of St Augustine. The Canongate was put under the jurisdiction of Holyrood Abbey by King David I. in 1128, the City of Edinburgh acquiring the superiority of the Burgh in 1636, incorporating it in the year 1856.

In 1769 the Canongate boasted among its residents two Dukes, sixteen Earls, seven Barons, seven Judges, thirteen Baronets. " When royalty went to London, nobility followed " (Alexander Smith). " The removal of the residence of the Sovereign has had the

PLATE XXVII

Coull's Close

W. Gibb

COULL'S CLOSE

See page 73

effect of rendering the great nobility of Scotland very indifferent about the capital " (*Peter's Letters*).

Cranston Street

This Street, formerly Leith Wynd, was the chief route by which travellers landing at Leith approached Edinburgh.

The Rev. Joseph Robertson, of the Chapel of Ease at the lower end of Leith Wynd, married the poet Shelley to Harriet Westbrook in August 1811. Neither was of the right age in England, so that the couple hied northward to Edinburgh. Shelley, " farmer, Sussex," occupied furnished rooms at William Cumming's, 60 George Street. The Rev. Joseph Robertson, whose private address was 225 Canongate, was banished from Scotland for conducting marriages illegally.

[Coull's Close]

At the lower end was " Paul's Work," where the Ballantyne Press printed the Waverley Novels. (In 1822 were published 145,000 volumes.) Scott, who knew James Ballantyne as a boy at Kelso, spoke of him on his removal to Edinburgh in 1802 " as a great critic as well as an excellent printer," and he spoke also of the two brothers " as my old friends and schoolfellows, the Ballantynes of Edinburgh." " Ballantyne continues to flourish like a green bay tree, but instead of being planted by a river, he has established at the bottom of Leith Wynd a hall equal to that which the Genii of the lamp built for Aladdin in point of size, but rather less superbly furnished, being occupied by about a dozen of presses."

Coull's has been traditionally the scene of what

K

Scott describes in *Rokeby*—the lodging to which the blindfolded divine was carried by sedan chair, in which he was compelled to pray as if the lady were dying, and from which he was hurrying when he heard the report of a pistol.

Rae's Close (281)

The builder, Rae, was a Royal barber and surgeon ; only a fragment of the building remains.

Morocco Close (273)

On the front of Morocco Land is displayed the figure of a Moor with turban and necklace. Tradition, perhaps unfounded, asserts that a student, Andrew Gray, had been arrested as ringleader of a disturbance at the home of an unpopular Provost. Gray escaped from the Edinburgh Tolbooth, went to sea, and rose to high rank in the household of the Emperor of Morocco. Many years afterwards (1645) a Moorish vessel lay at anchor in Leith Roads. The commander, Andrew Gray, inquiring for the Provost of his college days, learned that the daughter suffered from plague, and volunteered to cure her. The cure proving satisfactory, he married his patient, setting up house in what has since been called Morocco Land.

Seaton's Close (267)

The period to which this residence belongs is the eighteenth century, and Seaton is said to have served as surgeon with General Wade.

Kinloch's Close (265A)

Perhaps named after Kinloch of Gilmerton, Lord Provost in 1677. Sir Daniel Wilson names one

Henry Kinloch, who entertained the ambassadors come from France to invest Darnley with the Order of St Michael.

New Street

Here stood the house of Henry Home, Lord Kames (1696-1782), judge, philosopher, agriculturist. Speaking of Kames's essay on the *Elements of Criticism*, Goldsmith said that it was a book easier to write than to read. Kames was the judge who tried a certain Matthew Hay for murder at Ayr in 1780—they used to play at chess together. A verdict of guilty being returned, the judge exclaimed, —" That's checkmate for you, Matthew." Johnson had a poor opinion of Kames, and Scott describes him as " an acute, metaphysical judge, though somewhat coarse in his manners."

In a house more than half-way down New Street resided Sir David Dalrymple, Lord Hailes (1726-92), jurist and historian. He declined to revise for Hume his *Inquiry into the Human Mind*, and was one of those who censured the sceptic, then Keeper of the Advocate's Library, for purchasing certain objectionable French works. Boswell is said to have acquired from Hailes the desire to meet Johnson. Hailes's *magnum opus* is *The Annals of Scotland*. At Lord Hailes's Johnson and Boswell " spent a most agreeable day."

[Little Jack's Close]

Jack seems to have been a slater.

Here Susanna, Allan Ramsay's Countess of Eglintoun, entertained Prince Charles Edward and his suite in 1745, and here she resided in her old age, her favourite pastime being the taming of rats.

In this Close from 1753 to 1762 David Hume had his second Edinburgh home, and wrote the greater portion of his *History of England*. He gave suppers to his friends, assembling " whosoever were most knowing and agreeable among either the laity or the clergy." " For innocent mirth and agreeable raillery," says Alexander Carlyle, " I never knew his match."

Jack's Land lay between the " Jack " Closes. Behind Jack's Land stood the mansion of General Thomas Dalyell, of Binns. As an officer in the Russian Army against the Poles and the Turks, he had recourse to stern methods. Being appointed by King Charles II. Commander-in-Chief in Scotland, Dalyell defeated the Covenanters at Rullion Green (1666). " A man more feared and hated by the Whigs than even Claverhouse himself," he raised a regiment known to this day as the Scots Greys. He is remembered as having worn a breast-plate, " over which descended a gray beard of venerable length, which he cherished as a mark of mourning for Charles the First, having never shaved since that monarch was brought to the scaffold " (*Old Mortality*).

Shoemakers' Land (215)

Over the door of Cordiners' Land a tablet bears the arms of the Craft, the date 1677, the crown of the patron St Crispin, cherubs' heads, together with a rounding knife. An open book reveals the first verse of Psalm 133.

Cordiners' Land is named after " Cordiner " or " Cordwainer," a worker in Cordova leather. Of the fourteen incorporated trades of Edinburgh, the shoemakers ranked next in wealth to the goldsmiths.

PLATE XXVIII

SHOEMAKERS' LAND

See page 76

PLATE XXIX

CANONGATE TOLBOOTH

See page 77

The *Edinburgh Directory* (1773 to 1786) names as an inhabitant of the Close, Robert Oliphant of Rossie, Postmaster-General for Scotland.

Gladstone Court (181)

The former name was Bowling Green Close.

Tolbooth Wynd (165)

The building over the entrance is noteworthy.

Claverhouse usually occupied quarters in this vicinity.

Taylor, the Water-Poet, describing the Canongate, speaks of " buildings on each side of the way being all of squared stone, five, six, and seven stories high, and many by-lanes and closes on each side of the way, wherein are gentlemen's houses, much fairer than the buildings in the high street, for in the high street marchants and tradesmen do dwell, but the gentlemen's mansions and goodliest houses are obscurely founded in the aforesaid lanes ; the walles are eight or tenne foote thicke, exceeding strong, not built for a day, a weeke, or a moneth, or a yeere."

Canongate Tolbooth (163)

Built in 1591 in the Scoto-French style of architecture, the Tolbooth was the structure in which public dues or tolls were collected. The Council Chamber for many years, it was converted into the prison, but was discontinued in the beginning of 1848. Between 1661 and 1688 the cells were occupied by various Covenanters.

The " S.L.B." of one tablet may represent the initials of Sir Lewis Bellenden superior of the Canongate when the Tolbooth was erected. The other inscriptions read thus :—" For one's country and one's successors, 1591."—" King James VI. Justice and Piety are the strong bulwarks of a prince." The coat-of-arms of the Burgh bears a stag's head with a cross between the tynes, the Abbey of Holyrood owing its origin to a legendary incident connected with King David I. and an infuriated stag, from which he was protected by a cross from heaven. " Sic itur ad astra. ' This is the path to heaven.' Such," writes Scott in *Chronicles of the Canongate*, " is the ancient motto attached to the armorial bearings of the Canongate, which is inscribed, with greater or less propriety, upon all the public buildings, from the church to the pillory, in the ancient quarter of Edinburgh which bears, or rather once bore, the same relation to the Good Town as Westminster does to London, being still possessed of the palace of the sovereign, as it formerly was dignified by the residence of the principal noblity and gentry."

Canongate Church

The nave of Holyrood Abbey Church was used as the parish church of the Canongate from the period of the Reformation. The Order of the Thistle, instituted by King James V. about 1540, was renewed by King James VII. in 1687. The latter claimed the old conventual church " for his chapel Royal and had fitted up accordingly in a style of splendour which grievously outraged the feelings of his presbyterian subjects." The Canongate Church was founded in 1691 for the outed congregation, a bequest in 1649 by Thomas Moodie of Dalry providing the funds.

Until the present Church was opened, the

parishioners worshipped in Holyrood Abbey, the old register having the customary quaint entries. For instance, in 1565 on March 9, " Monsr Sengnior David ves slane in Holyrodhuse," and July 29, " Henry and Marie Kyng and Qwene of Scottis were married," while the entry of February 10, 1566 runs—" the Kyngs grace blawen up with buder in the Kirk of Field."

The private soldiers who were taken prisoners by Charles Edward Stuart at Prestonpans were confined " in the Jail and Church of Canongate." The *Caledonian Mercury* described the Prince at that time as a man " who could eat a dry crust, sleep on peas straw, take his dinner in four minutes, and win a battle in five."

Four communion cups and four carved chairs, with the baptismal plate, and the clock seem to have been brought from Holyroodhouse.

Among the eminent ministers of the Canongate Church was John Lee, D.D. (1779-1859), after-wards Principal of Edinburgh University, the " Archdeacon Meadow " of *The Book Hunter*. Before being examined by a Committee of the House of Commons, Lee " suddenly disappeared with all his money in his pocket, and returned penniless, followed by a waggon containing 372 copies of rare editions of the Bible."

SOME OF THE TOMBS OF THE CHURCHYARD

1. George Drummond (1687-1766) ; six times Lord Provost of Edinburgh (twelve years in all).

2. Adam Smith, LL.D. (1723-90) ; author of *The Wealth of Nations*. Here lies his relative Lord Reston, one of Walter Scott's companions at the High School.

3. Professor James Gregory, M.D. (1753-1821) ; com-pounder of Gregory's Mixture.

4. Robert Keith (1681-1757) ; Bishop Keith it was who in 1746 married Jean daughter of the 2nd Marquess of Douglas to Sir John Stewart of Grandtully, Bart. By the decision of " the great Douglas cause " Jean's surviving son succeeded to the Douglas estates, and was eventually created Lord Douglas. Bishop of Fife, historian.

5. George Chalmers (1773-1836) ; plumber, founder of Chalmers Hospital.

6. Alexander Runciman (1736-85) ; historical painter. Monument erected by the Royal Scottish Academy to commemorate him and his brother John who died at Naples.

7. Robert Fergusson ; poet. " Burns's master in his art, who died insane while yet a stripling " (R.L.S.). " By special grant of the Managers to Robert Burns, who erected this stone, this burial-place is to remain for ever sacred to the memory of Robert Fergusson." Burns paid £5, 10s. for the monument.

8. Alexander Brunton, D.D. (1772-1854) ; Professor of Hebrew. His wife wrote " Self-Control " and " Discipline."

9. James Ramsay (1624-96) ; Bishop of Dunblane and Ross.

10. Dugald Stewart (1753-1828) ; Professor of Moral Philosophy.

11. Sir Patrick Hume, 1st Earl of Marchmont (1641-1724) ; opposing Lauderdale's drastic measures against the Covenanters, concealed himself in the vault of Polwarth Church, and was there fed by the daughter Lady Grizel Baillie.

12. John Frederick Lampe (1703-51) ; bassoon player : conducted orchestra in Canongate Theatre.

13. Lord Provost Sir William Fettes, Bart. (1750-1836) ; founder of Fettes College.

14. John Ballantyne (1774-1821) ; printer. Scott whispered to Lockhart at the graveside on John Ballantyne's funeral day :—" I feel as if there would be less sunshine for me from this day forth."

15. James Ballantyne (1772-1833) ; printer ; buried " close in front of Fettes's tomb-gate."

16. Hugh W. Williams (1773-1829) ; " Grecian Williams," landscape painter. " Dear, delightful Williams " (Christopher North).

17. Sir John Watson Gordon, R.A. (1788-1864) ; portrait painter, Raeburn's successor in Scotland.

18. Horatius Bonar, D.D. (1808-89) ; hymn writer.

19. " Clarinda "—Mrs Maclehose (1759-1841), who corresponded with Burns (" Sylvander "). The letters formed, in Scott's opinion, " the most extraordinary mixture of sense and nonsense, and of love human and divine, that was ever exposed to the eye of the world." " Take her for all in all, I believe she was the best woman Burns encountered " (R.L.S.). She died at 14 Calton Hill, and lies in the tomb of her relative, the Scots judge, Lord Craig.

20. Robert Forsyth (1764-1845) ; author of *The Beauties of Scotland*.

21. Benjamin Bell, surgeon, great-grandfather of " Sherlock Holmes " (Dr Joseph Bell).

22. John Irving, W.S. (1770-1850) ; " in boyhood the chosen friend of Walter Scott."

23. Luke Fraser (1736-1821) ; Scott, who was a pupil of his in the High School, calls him " a good Latin scholar and a very worthy man."

24. Riccio's mutilated body is said to have been interred under the Chapel passage at Holyroodhouse, but the remains of the Secretary were exhumed and reburied, says tradition, under the carved stone at the south-east corner of the Canongate Church.

Dunbar's Close (137)

Mrs Love had her celebrated oyster cellar near the Canongate Church. When Burns was in Edinburgh, ladies of fashion wearing masks frequented Mrs Love's, " eating oysters and drinking punch and porter." Her son, Kenneth Love, " tyler " to the members of Lodge Canongate Kilwinning, No. 2, figures in Stuart Watson's

L

" Meeting of the Members." " Most of those
oyster cellars have a sort of long room, where a
small party may enjoy the exercise of a country
dance, to the music of a fiddle, harp, or bag-pipe "
(Arnot, *History of Edinburgh*).

Panmure Close (129)

Here resided Maule of Panmure, Forfarshire.
James, the 4th Earl, remained faithful to King
James VII. after the latter's flight to France, and
at the Convention of the Estates opposed the
recognition of William and Mary. He proclaimed
the Old Chevalier King at the Cross of Brechin in
1715, entertaining him at Brechin Castle the following
year. In June 1746 Panmure was attainted, and the
estates confiscated. The house was occupied later
by a Countess of Aberdeen.

The father of political economy, Adam Smith,
occupied the residence from 1778 to 1790. He
owed his appointment in 1777 as one of the Commissioners of Customs to the suggestions which
he made about taxes in *The Wealth of Nations*,
published the previous year. The work argues that
every man promotes the interests of his fellows by
attending to his own. The publication was first
mentioned in the Commons by Fox. Adam Smith
once met Pitt, Addington, and Grenville at Henry
Dundas's at dinner. When the great Scotsman
entered, the company rose. " Be seated, gentlemen,"
said he. Pitt requested Smith to be seated first,
" for we are all your scholars." One Sunday evening
the economist was entertaining some friends to
supper at Panmure House. Looking ill, he was
advised to retire early. Pausing with his hand on
the door, he addressed the guests :—" I fear I shall

PLATE XXX

BROWN'S COURT

See page 84

PLATE XXXI

JANET HALL'S ALEHOUSE

See page 84

never meet you again, but I trust we shall meet in another, a better world." Next Saturday he was dead.

Little Lochend Close (115)

Here Mrs Hannah Robertson, reputed granddaughter of King Charles II., entertained persons with Jacobite sympathies.

Campbell's Close (87)

Spiral stair.

In Campbell's Land have resided Arthur Ross, Archbishop of St Andrews and the 13th as well as the 14th Earl of Morton.

From these flats one sees the Calton Cemetery, where, near the east wall, rest the parents of Robert Louis Stevenson.

> There, on the sunny frontage of a hill,
> Hard by the house of kings, repose the dead,
> My dead, the ready and the strong of word.

Allan Ramsay wrote an elegy on " Luckie " Wood, the respected keeper of an alehouse in this part of the Canongate. On the departure of the Scots Members of Parliament to London after the Union, her house fell on evil days.

> O Canigate ! puir elritch hole,
> What loss, what crosses does thou thole !
> London an' death gars thee look droll,
> An' hing thy heid !

Golfer's Land (81)

Two members of an English Golf Club, attached to the suite of the Duke of York (afterwards King James VII.), were challenged by the Duke to a match on Leith Links, his partner being a shoemaker, John Patersone. The match was duly played, His Royal Highness and Patersone being the winners. The stakes enabled Patersone to build Golfer's Land.

One notes the armorial, as well as the tablet on which the incident is described in Latin by Dr Archibald Pitcairne (1652-1713). The anagram for " John Patersone " is appended :—" I hate no person."

[Brown's Court]

The old house had an attractive stair-case.

Callender's Entry (67)

The Callenders were blacksmiths under Royal patronage.

Janet Hall's alehouse in this Entry was noted for its claret. John Gay (1685-1732), poet, dramatist, author of *The Beggar's Opera*, came to Edinburgh with his patrons, the 3rd Duke of Queensberry and the Duchess. The poet told Swift that he accompanied his great friends wheresoever they would carry him. Gay frequented " Janet Hall's " with Alan Ramsay and other wits. " Tradition in Edinburgh used to point out an attic in an old house opposite to Queensberry House, where, as an appropriate abode for a poet, his patrons are said to have stowed him " (Chambers).

Whitefoord House (53)

The Scottish Naval and Military Veterans' Residence occupies the site of " My Lord Seyton's Lodging," to which Roland Graeme pursued Catherine Seyton after one of the street skirmishes then common in Edinburgh. "The page entered with the same precipitation as had marked his whole proceeding and found himself in a large gloomy hall or vestibule, dimly enlightened by lattice casements of painted glass, and rendered yet dimmer through the exclusion of the sunbeams, owing to the height of the walls of those buildings by which the courtyard was enclosed. The walls of the hall were surrounded with suits of ancient and rusted armour, interchanged with huge and massive stone scutcheons, bearing double tressures, fleured and counter fleured wheat sheaves, coronets, and so forth—things to which Roland Graeme gave not a moment's attention " (*The Abbot*).

George, the 5th Lord Seton (1530-85), Provost of Edinburgh, acted as host to Queen Mary and Darnley at Seton during their honeymoon. After the murder of Riccio, Seton accompanied the Royal couple first to Seton, thence to Dunbar. To Seton the Queen repaired after Darnley's assassination. Robert, the 6th Lord Seton, a favourite with King James VI., was created Earl of Winton. Dying in 1603, he was buried the very day the King left Edinburgh for London. " As James was trooping towards England, bag and baggage, his journey was stopped near Cockenzie by meeting the funeral of the Earl of Winton, the old and faithful servant and follower of his ill-fated mother, poor Mary " (*Chronicles of the Canongate*).

George, the 5th Earl of Winton (d. 1749), whom Mackay describes in *Secret Memoirs* as " a young gentleman who hath been much abroad in the world," was made prisoner at the battle of Preston ; alone of the earls tried for treason during the Rising of 1715, he refused to plead guilty. Sentenced to death, he made his escape from the Tower, went to France, and died in Rome.

Whitefoord House seems to have derived its name from Sir John Whitefoord, Bart. (d. 1803), who purchased the property on leaving Ballochmyle, Ayrshire. He is believed to have been " Sir Arthur Wardour " of *The Antiquary*—a country gentleman who " hunted and fished, gave and received dinners, attended races and country meetings, was a deputy-lieutenant and trustee upon turnpike acts." To Sir John it was that Burns sent his *Lament on Lord Glencairn*.

Whitehorse Close (31)

Anxious to make peace with the Covenanters, King Charles I. proclaimed in 1639 that the religion of Scotland would be safe in his hands. When money was beginning to run short, and the King was at Berwick, he realised that his army would soon break up, and he thereupon sent to Edinburgh for the Lords of the Covenanting party. They met in the Whitehorse Close, mounted their horses to ride to the King, all being checked by the mob except Montrose, now a Royalist.

The Bishops of Edinburgh, who had St Giles's as their cathedral, from 1633 to 1690, were William Forbes, David Lindsay, George Wishart, Alexander Young, John Paterson, and Alexander Rose. One of the houses in Whitehorse Close was occupied by John Paterson (1632-1708) and Alexander Rose (1647-1720). Paterson, who rose to be Archbishop of Glasgow, owed his promotion to the Duchess of Lauderdale. In company with " Bloody " Mackenzie, Alexander Rose travelled to Whitehall in 1689 to be received in audience by King William III.

PLATE XXXII

WHITEHORSE CLOSE

See page 86

Plate XXXIII

Boyd's Close

See page 90

Understanding that the bulk of the aristocracy in Scotland were in favour of episcopacy, the King expressed the hope that Bishop Rose would follow the example of England. The prelate answered :— " Sir, I will serve you so far as law, reason, or conscience will allow me."

Whitehorse Close contained " the inn or hostelry of St Michael, which stood," says *The Abbot*, " in a large courtyard off the main street, close under the descent of the Calton Hill." Thither Roland Graeme repaired with the falconer of Avenel, Adam Woodcock. " It was a busy scene, for the number of gentlemen and nobles who were now crowded into the city had filled all spare stables and places of public reception with their horses and military attendants." The minstrel's instrument " had drawn in several auditors from the street," among them Henry Seyton, whose form and face Graeme mistook for those of the sister Catherine, and who handed Graeme a sword to unsheathe before the rightful sovereign only.

The same hostelry served as the meeting place of Edward Waverley and Fergus MacIvor—" a small paved court, retiring from the street called the Canongate, at the house of a buxom widow of forty." Mrs Flockhart, " smiling in her weeds like the sun through a mist, took the head of the table, thinking within herself, perhaps, that she cared not how long the rebellion lasted that brought her into company so much above her usual associates. She was supported by Waverley and the Baron with the advantage of the Chieftain, vis-a-vis " (*Waverley*).

While the Whitehorse Close was being restored, the date over the prominent dormer window was changed to 1632, although *Views in Edinburgh* by

Storer makes the year 1683, a date said to be in keeping with the architecture.

On the north is Calton Road, where stand eight of the arches of the old stables and coach-houses, with " smithy." From this place started the coaches for Newcastle and London. Scott instances the case of a single letter constituting the mail from London (1737).

ABBEY STRAND—North Side

Thomson's Court (9)

In the quaint building, recently restored, aristo-cratic debtors found sanctuary.

Here lived in the eighteenth century a notorious character, Luckie Spence, satirised by Allan Ramsay :—

> Lass, gi'e us in anither gill,
> A mutchken, jo, let's tak our fill ;
> Let Death syne registrate his bill
>   When I want sense,
> I'll slip away with better will,
>   Quo' Lucky Spence.

" Mr Chrystal Croftangry," a debtor within the precincts, lodged with " an honest Highland-woman," Janet McEvoy, the " undisputed owner of one flat of a small tenement in the Abbey Yard."

When later he returned to Auld Reekie, he went says he, " to the very portion of the Canongate in which I had formerly been immured, like the errant knight, prisoner in some enchanted castle, where spells have made the ambient air impervious to the unhappy captive, although the organs of sight

Plate XXXIV

Old Playhouse Close

See page 91

PLATE XXXV

MORAY HOUSE

See page 94

encountered no obstacle to his free passage "
(*Chronicles of the Canongate*).

The " Houses of Refuge," distant from Holyroodhouse a hundred yards or more and separated
from the Burgh of Canongate by a paved girth,
with the brass letter " S," were occupied by debtors
who had here the right of sanctuary. The " Baron
Bailie," as he was styled, settled disputes, even
sending refugees to jail. The sanctuary dwellers
(" Abbey lairds ") were permitted to cross the girth
on Sunday only.

Among the debtors who availed themselves of
this retreat was De Quincey. His wife died there.

It is a pleasing reflection that while one Sanctuary
has disappeared amidst general satisfaction, another
with equal satisfaction has come into being—the
Bird Sanctuary at Duddingston.

CANONGATE—South Side

From " Wastle's " own house, " the way thither
lies straight down the only great street of the Old
Town—a street by far the most impressive in its
character of any I have ever seen in Britain "
(Lockhart).

St Mary's Street
This Street or Wynd, immediately outside the
City Wall, was named after a nunnery dedicated to
the Virgin Mary. The Red Lion or Ramsay's Inn,
with accommodation for 100 horses and 20 carriages,
was perhaps named after Peter Ramsay, brother of
William Ramsay, the first laird of Barnton, and a
prominent sporting character. Pascal Paoli, Corsican

patriot, and personal friend of the Johnsonian group, arrived at the Inn in 1771, subsequently going to James's Court as the guest of Boswell.

[Boyd's Close]

James Boyd's Inn, at the sign of the White Horse, is not to be confused with the other hostelry in the Whitehorse Close at the lower end of the Canongate. Johnson arrived at Boyd's on Saturday, August 14, 1773. The house was then kept by a woman called " Luckie," a word synonymous with " Goody." The accommodation was not inconsiderable ; there were 13 bedrooms and there was stabling for 50 horses. Johnson " asked to have his lemonade made sweeter ; upon which," according to Boswell, " the waiter, with his greasy fingers, lifted a lump of sugar, and put it into it. The Doctor, in indignation, threw it out of the window."

Johnson and Boswell walked arm-in-arm to the latter's house in James's Court.

Gullan's Close (264), Gibb's Close (250)

The old buildings in this vicinity are worth preserving.

One of the three specific charges against the murderer Burke was, that in Gibb's Close at the house of his brother, Constantine, scavenger, he strangled Mary Paterson, an unfortunate.

Chessels Court (240)

Built by Andrew Chessels. Here stands the old Excise Office, the scene of the last exploit of Deacon Brodie, when he stole some £16. The railing in front is of wrought iron. The last tenement on the right has a noticeable balustrade.

Plainstone Close (222)

The original Close had been paved with flagstones instead of causeway stones or cobbles.

Miln's Close (212)

Cromwell's sick and wounded soldiers were quartered here : during recent excavations skeletons have been discovered.

Weir's Close (206)

The houses between this Close and Miln's date back a century or two.

Playhouse Close (200)

The foundation-stone having been laid by the London actor, John Ryan, in 1746, the Theatre was opened in 1747. It had a double row of dormer windows which provided light for the dressing-rooms. Handel's bassoon player (Lampe) was for a time leader of the orchestra. The Canongate Theatre ceased to exist in 1786, the year in which the Theatre Royal was opened at Shakespeare Square (the site of the present General Post Office).

" The Man of Feeling " once saw the future King Charles X., Count d'Artois (1757-1836), " wrapped in an old surtout, accompanied only by his favourite M. de Puysegur, in a little dirty close in the Canongate where they had been looking at some old house (I believe the old Theatre) " ; Mackenzie adds that he almost wept to think of his reduced state.

Old Playhouse Close (196)

To this Close, Hugh Miller, geologist and journalist, was led by a ragged child to see Mary

Duff, who years before had been " bred up beside him in Cromarty," and who was now in destitution. Miller slipped half-a-crown into Mary's hand, promising he would call again in the morning ; Mary died that night.   At the funeral in the Canongate Churchyard he met an old woman to whom Margaret an hour before her death had given the half-crown in payment of a debt.   This incident is the subject of John Brown's *Her Last Half-Crown.*

St John's Close (188)

Here is situated Lodge Canongate Kilwinning, No. 2, the organ built in 1757 being still in use. In Stuart Watson's picture of the imaginary meeting of the Lodge, when Robert Burns is reputed to have been made Poet Laureate, appear eminent members.   Twenty years elapsed before the Minute-Book proclaimed that Burns had been Laureate of the Lodge.

Practically opposite St John's Close stood St John's Cross (indicated by a ring of cobble-stones). There King James VI. knighted Provost William Nisbet in 1617 ; there King Charles I. knighted Provost Alexander Clerk in 1634 ; and there King Charles II. knighted and conferred on Provost Sir Andrew Ramsay in 1667 the title of Lord Provost, Ramsay having already got a knighthood from Cromwell.

The City of Edinburgh seems to have claimed the south side of the Canongate from the Netherbow to St John's Cross.   The portion mentioned having already belonged to Edinburgh, the City acquired superiority over the rest of the Burgh of Canongate in 1636.

St John's Street

This private street which was begun in 1768 used to be guarded by a steward in uniform. Only houses Nos. 1-6 are extant. The house with the arch was that of the Earl of Hopetoun. The first floor was occupied by Mrs Telfer in 1766, when she entertained her brother Tobias Smollett, M.D. (1721-71). He had been elected a Burgess and Guild Brother of Edinburgh six years before, and during his second visit met some men of distinction, among them David Hume, John Home, Principal Robertson, Adam Smith, Hugh Blair. Referring to Smollett's first visit to Scotland, Jupiter Carlyle writes :—" He came out to Musselburgh and passed a day and a night with me, and went to church and heard me preach."

South of Lodge Canongate Kilwinning, No. 2, is the former residence of the Earl of Wemyss.

At No. 3 St John's Street lived the Rev. Dr Alexander Brunton (1772-1854), Professor of Hebrew, and his talented wife Mary (1778-1818).

At No. 8 resided Sir David Rae, Lord Eskgrove (1724-1804), who succeeded Braxfield as Lord Justice-Clerk. Eskgrove was one of the judges who tried Deacon Brodie (1788), and the Parliamentary Reformers (1794). Later at No. 8 resided the Countess of Hyndford. She, the eldest daughter and heiress of William Grant of Prestongrange, was the widow of John, the 4th Earl of Hyndford.

At No. 10 James Ballantyne (1772-1833), Scott's printer, who was wont to give a " gorgeous " feast to his intimate friends on the eve of the issue of a novel by the Great Unknown, and to read from the proof-sheets particularly striking passages.

At No. 12 Robert Ainslie, W.S., Burns's companion in the Border Tour of 1787.

At No. 13 the judge, James Burnett, Lord Monboddo (1714-99). "Classical learning, good conversation, excellent suppers, and ingenious though unsound metaphysics, were the peculiarities of Monboddo" (Cockburn). During the sittings of the Court, he gave a "learned supper" once a fortnight, Robert Burns frequently being his guest. Monboddo's daughter, "the fair Burnett" of the Poet's song, died of tuberculosis at the age of twenty-two.

At No. 15 Dr John Gregory (1725-73), father of James compounder of Gregory's Mixture. Dr John was professor of medicine at Aberdeen from 1756 to 1764. In 1764 he removed to Edinburgh, being elected to the Chair of Practice of Physic in 1766. He entertained the poet, Gray in 1765.

In St John's Street resided members of such families as Blantyre, Allanbank, Ashestiel, Seggieden, Mortonhall, Baberton.

Canongate (184)

The florists' shop of to-day is reputed to have been one of the two original places of business possessed by John Lawson Johnston, butcher and poulterer. He it was who, according to the son George, 1st Baron Luke of Pavenham, invented "Bovril" in Canada about 1875, and who brought the material to London ten years later.

Moray House (174)

This mansion has no connection with the "Good Regent" Moray, but was erected in King Charles I.'s reign (about 1628 by Mary Sutton, widow of the 1st

Earl of Home, at whose death it passed to her daughter, Margaret, wife of the 4th Earl of Moray. It has exquisitely beautiful ceilings and wood-carving.

David Buchanan (1595-1652), who wrote a description of Edinburgh in Latin to accompany Gordon of Rothiemay's Plan of the City, described the residence and gardens of the Earl as " of such elegance, and cultivated with such diligence, that they easily challenge comparison with the gardens of warmer climates and almost of England itself, and here you may see how much human skill and industry avail in making up for the defects of nature herself."

At Lady Home's " Lodging " in the Canongate Cromwell put up on one occasion. He seems to have spent a night in Moray House, and to have resided for nearly a year in the citadel of Leith.

The festivities being continued for a few days after the marriage of Lady Mary Stuart, daughter of the 4th Lord Moray, to Lord Lorne, afterwards the 9th Earl of Argyll, the chief guests assembled on May 18, 1650 on the corbelled balcony to see Montrose pass, " bound to the cart with a rope." Montrose was being taken to the Parliament House, " there, in the place of delinquents, on his knees to receive his sentence." The Marquess of Argyll and his son (the bridegroom of 1650) were themselves executed at the Cross, the one in 1661, the other in 1685 ; the former suffered " for his horrid villainies against King Charles the martyr."

James Ogilvy, the 1st Earl of Seafield (1664-1730), tenanted Moray House at the time of the Union with England. He was the last Lord High Chancellor of Scotland, a minister vested with the authority and

power of a viceroy. In dismissing the last Scots
Parliament, he exclaimed, " Now there's ane end of
ane auld sang." Mrs Bethune Baliol (*Chronicles of
the Canongate*) says that from the balcony in front
of Lord Moray's Lodging her mother saw " the
riding of the last Scottish Parliament."

A summer-house has been erected by Lord
Guthrie on the spot where some of the signatures
were obtained for the Union.

Huntly House (174)

Evidence is wanting that the mansion was the
property of the Huntly family.

The first Marquess (1562-1636), who slew the
bonnie Earl of Moray, had a lodging somewhere in
the Canongate, and Henrietta, daughter of Lord
Peterborough and widow of the 2nd Duke of Gordon,
tenanted in 1750 a portion of the property in Bakehouse Close.

Apropos of the 'Fifteen the Minute-Book (January
25, 1720) mentions some thirty-four persons, including " Jean Baillie, Lady Castlecarie," who,
" seized and apprehended within the lodgings of
the Dutchess Dowager of Gordon as Papists, and
assembled together for wirshop, were thereafter
committed to the Canongate Prison."

The timber-fronted gables are worthy of notice.
The Latin mottoes read :—

Another hope of life.

To a constant spirit the things of mortals
are as a shadow.

As you are master of your tongue, so
am I master of my ears.

To-day for me, to-morrow for you, why worry ?   1570.

PLATE XXXVI

HUNTLY HOUSE

See page 69

PLATE XXXVII

ACHESON'S DOORWAY

See page 97

Bakehouse Close (146)

Here the Incorporation of Bakers possessed property.

Down the Close is the residence of the Acheson family with forecourt, dormer windows, and crow-stepped gable. Over the doorway is a cock perched on a trumpet, with the motto *Vigilantibus 1633*. The initials S. A. A. denote Sir Archibald Acheson, Solicitor-General, Senator of College of Justice, Secretary of State,—D. M. H. his second wife, Dame Margaret Hamilton, grandchild of Lord Paisley (of the House of Abercorn). Sir Archibald was an ancestor of the Earls of Gosford.

" When I heard her carry her description of manners so far back beyond her own time," Croftangry refers to conversations on the Canongate with Mrs Bethune Baliol, " and describe how Fletcher of Saltoun spoke, how Grahame of Claverhouse danced, what were the jewels worn by the famous Duchess of Lauderdale and how she came by them, I could not help telling her I thought her some fairy, who cheated us by retaining the appearance of a mortal of our own day, when in fact she had witnessed the revolutions of centuries."

Wilson's Court (134)

The group of dwellings is old. An excellent view can be had from the windows of the spiral stair. Note the ancient buildings in the rear of Slater's and in front of Bakehouse Close. Gratings were used for the windows to prevent stuff from being cast therefrom.

Gentle's Close

It is named after James Gentle, brewer, from

N

whom Burns asked leave to erect the stone on the grave of Robert Fergusson.

Bull's Close (106)

From this Close one sees Salisbury Crags. " Yes, Edina, thou art indeed a noble city, a metropolis worthy of the land of mountain and of flood, glen, forest, loch, and long-winding arms of ocean ! Queen of the North ! which of thy august shrines dost thou love the best—the Castle-cliff, within whose hoary battlements Kings were born— the Green Hill looking down on deserted Holyrood— the Crags smitten into grandeur and beauty by time and the elements—or the Mountain, like a lion couchant, reposing in the sky ? " (" Christopher North," *Noctes Ambrosianae*).

Milton House (School) (90)

The school as viewed from the south is imposing. Portions of the old walls of Milton House have been preserved.

According to Edgar's Map the Duke of Roxburghe lived here in 1742. The mansion was occupied some twenty years later by Andrew Fletcher, Lord Milton (1692-1766), nephew of Fletcher of Saltoun, who died lamenting the Union of 1707. When 32 years of age Fletcher became a judge, succeeding Erskine of Grange as Lord Justice-Clerk and presiding in 1736 at the trial of Captain John Porteous. Jupiter Carlyle, speaking of Lord Milton as political manager of this country under Argyll, says of him :—" He was a man of great ability in business, a man of good sense, and of excellent talents for managing men." Milton is said to have abstained from severe measures during the Rising of 1745 and to have " adopted means either to conceal or to recall such of the rebels as had been misled from the paths of loyalty."

Haddington's Entry and Reid's Close (80)

The residence over the Canongate arch was that of Sir John Nisbet, Lord Dirleton (1609-87), "one of the most learned men of his age." He was the last Lord Advocate with a seat on the bench. As prosecutor of the unfortunate Presbyterians, he nearly equalled in severity his successor, Sir George Mackenzie. Gilbert Burnet characterises Dirleton as "a man of great learning both in law and in many other things, chiefly in the Greek learning; he was a person of great integrity; only he loved money too much, but he always stood firm to the law."

Reid's Close used to have the eighteenth-century residence of the Earl of Aberdeen, one room of which had mural paintings; (on the left) at the end of Haddington's Entry resided the Earl of Haddington.

Queensberry House (64)

Now a House of Refuge for the Destitute, it was built in the reign of King Charles II. by the judge Lord Halton, Charles Maitland, afterwards 3rd Earl of Lauderdale (d. 1691). The mansion was sold to William, the 1st Duke of Queensberry (1637-95), and held by his successors until 1803. A floor has been added to the original structure. The 2nd Duke (1662-1711) was entrusted with completing the Treaty of Union, a duty which rendered his name unpopular throughout Scotland.

While signatures were being appended, Lord Drumlanrig, the heir, was left in Queensberry

House with a Canongate spit-boy. Drumlanrig, an idiot, murdered and roasted the boy !

A famous occupant of the house was the 3rd Duchess, Lady Catherine Hyde (1700-77), daughter of the Earl of Clarendon. She was beautiful, witty, kindly, but somewhat eccentric. She exercised no little influence over Pitt, and enjoyed the friendship of Congreve, Thomson, Pope, Prior, Swift. When Gay was refused a licence for the production of his opera *Polly*, the Queensberrys sheltered him for the rest of his life.

In Queensberry House were confined the officers of Cope's Army taken prisoner at Prestonpans ; after some days they were liberated on parole and allowed to lodge in the City.

Sir James Montgomery, baronet (1721-1803), author of the Entail Act which bears his name, lived in Queensberry House, and, " I believe," says Cockburn, " was the last gentleman who resided in that historical mansion, which, though now one of the asylums of destitution, was once the brilliant abode of rank and fashion and political intrigue. I wish the Canongate could be refreshed again by the habitual sight of the Lord Chief Baron's family and company, and the gorgeous carriage, and the tall and well-dressed figure, in the old style, of his Lordship himself."

Queensberry House was once a barrack ; the perpendicular rain-water pipe bears the date 1810.

Chancellor's Court (opposite Whitehorse Close)

Here stood the house of James Drummond (1648-1716), Lord Chancellor. He enjoyed the confidence of King James VII., becoming the chief agent in the Catholic administration of Scotland during the

PLATE XXXVIII

PALACE OF HOLYROODHOUSE

See page 103

Revolution, and being created Duke of Perth. He is notorious as having added the thumbscrew to the world's instruments of torture.

Horse Wynd

The old entrance to the Royal Stables.

Behind the eighteenth-century mansion, recognised by the vases on the roof, stood Lothian Hut, built by the 3rd Marquess of Lothian. It was the abode of Dugald Stewart, whom Scott regarded as " most impressive and eloquent," and whom Cockburn termed " the last of his illustrious class." When Stewart lectured on Political Economy, his audience would include Sydney Smith, Francis Horner, Lord Jeffrey, Henry Erskine, Lord Brougham, Sir Archibald Alison, Lord John Russell.

Palmerston, a lad of 16, boarded with Dugald Stewart.

Across the roadway stretches the girth, with the letter " S " denoting Sanctuary, in which place of refuge the debtor could keep the creditors at bay. A few yards west from this point stood the " Girth Cross," the boundary of the Abbey Sanctuary, or—according to David Buchanan in his description of Edinburgh (1647-52)—" the Cross of the Precincts, because between it and the Abbey a certain space is marked off, which was formerly kept as an asylum for those who dared not venture abroad on account of the rigour of the law or the injustice of the supreme law." Scott abridges from Maitland the limits of what was the debtor's place of refuge until 1880, when imprisonment for debt was in most cases abolished : " One would think the space sufficiently extensive for a man to stretch his limbs in, as besides a reasonable proportion of level ground, considering that the scene lies in Scotland, it includes within its precincts the mountain of Arthurs Seat, and the rocks and pasture land called Salisbury Crags. But yet it is inexpressible how, after a certain time had elapsed, I used to long for Sunday, which permitted me to extend my walk without limitation. During the six other days of the week I felt a sickness of heart which, but for the speedy approach of the hebdomadal day of liberty, I could hardly have endured. I experienced the impatience of a mastiff, who tugs in vain to extend the limits which his chain permits " (*Chronicles of the Canongate*).

At the Girth Cross, on July 1, 1600, Jean Livingston, a beauty of nineteen, daughter of the Laird of Dunipace, was beheaded for the murder of her husband, John Kincaid of Wariston. She induced her father's servant, Robert Weir, to creep into Kincaid's bedroom and strangle him. It was the husband's cruelty which led Jean to seek his destruction.

ABBEY STRAND—South Side

Abbey Court-house (2)

The wall bears traces of the Gothic Porch erected in 1502 and demolished in 1753 by the Hereditary Keeper of the Palace, the 6th Duke of Hamilton.

Roland Graeme and Adam Woodcock " checked their horses, where the huge old vaulted entrance to the Abbey or Palace of Holyrood crossed the termination of the street, down which they had proceeded. The court-yard of the Palace opened within this gloomy porch, showing the front of an irregular pile of monastic buildings, one wing of which is still extant, forming a part of the modern palace, erected in the days of Charles II." (*The Abbot*).

" We boast being the court end of the town, possessing the Palace and the sepulchral remains of monarchs ; and we have the power to excite, in a degree unknown to the less-honoured quarters of the city, the dark and solemn recollections of ancient grandeur which occupied the precincts of our venerable Abbey from the time of St David " (*Fair Maid of Perth*).

PALACE OF HOLYROODHOUSE

Holyrood is " a house of many memories. Great people of yore, kings and queens, buffoons and grave ambassadors, played their stately farce for centuries in Holyrood. Wars have been plotted, dancing has lasted deep into the night, murder has been done in its chambers " (R. L. Stevenson).

Tradition says that King David I. founded the original building in 1128 as a thank-offering for his deliverance from an infuriated stag. The Monastery was converted after the Reformation into a Royal residence. The North-West Tower, begun by King James IV. in 1501, was completed by King James V. ; the remainder of the Palace, designed by Sir William Bruce of Kinross and founded in 1671 by Robert Mylne, Royal Master Mason, was erected by Lauderdale acting for King Charles II.

That North-West Tower contains the suite of apartments associated with Mary Stuart, John Knox, and David Riccio. The bed is not that of Mary Queen of Scots, however ; it is named after the

Mary of Modena, whom James Duke of York married in 1673.

The Picture Gallery is hung with fanciful portraits of sovereigns, all painted by one man, the Flemish artist, James de Witt. In the same apartment are exquisite panels by Hugo van der Goes from the altar-piece of Trinity College Church. Here it was that Prince Charles Edward gave the ball which Scott describes in *Waverley*. The Young Chevalier, when in Edinburgh, never appeared in a kilt, always dressed in tartan coat and breeches, never danced, and never slept in the Palace.

Here are elected the Scottish representative peers.

The first sovereign crowned in the Palace of Holyroodhouse was James II., the last, Charles I. The residence is occupied from time to time by Their Majesties, and during the sitting of the General Assembly of the Church of Scotland by the King's Representative, the Lord High Commissioner.

Situated in the south-east corner of the ruined Chapel—the nave of the Abbey Church—is the Royal vault with the remains of King David II. (1324-71); King James II. (1430-60) and Queen Mary of Gueldres; King James V. (1512-42) and Queen Madeline de Valois; Henry Lord Darnley (1545-67).

Among the celebrities who rest in the ancient pile are the following :—

David Dunbar, who married (1669) " Lucy Ashton," heroine of *The Bride of Lammermoor*.
Isabella Countess of Erroll (1742-1808), hostess of Johnson and Boswell at Slains Castle in 1773.
Miss Nicky Murray, directress of the Edinburgh dancing assemblies.

PLATE XXXIX

HOLYROOD ABBEY

See page 104

PLATE XL

HOLYROODHOUSE SUNDIAL

See page 105

Adam Bothwell (1527-93), Bishop of Orkney, who married Queen Mary and Lord Bothwell according to Presbyterian form.

William Hamilton of Bangour (1704-54), poet, whose admirers included Fergusson and Wordsworth.

Sir John Sinclair, of Ulbster (1784-1835), who carried out the *Statistical Account of Scotland*.

Thomas Lyon-Bowes (1773-1846) the 11th Earl of Strathmore. His son, Lord Glamis, had the chief share in entertaining the exiled French monarch Charles X. Fourth in descent from the 11th Earl are Lady Elphinstone and Queen Elizabeth.

The Royal Gardens boast a Charles I. Sun-Dial, Built by the Royal Master Mason in 1633, and bearing the initials of King Charles I., Queen Henrietta Maria, and the Prince of Wales.

INDEX

The names of places which no longer exist are in square brackets.

A

Abbey Court-house, 102
Advocate's Cl., 36
[Allan's Cl.], 38
Anchor Cl., 41
Assembly Hall, Free Church, 19
    do.   General, 7

B

Bailie Fyfe's Cl., 49
Bakehouse Cl., 97
[Bank Cl., New], 54
[do.   Old], 25
Bank Street, 17
[Baxter's Cl.], 16
Bell Close, 6
Bell's Wynd, 60
Bishop Bothwell's House, 34
Bishop's Cl., 47
Blackfriars Street, 66
[Blair's Cl.], 8
Borthwick's Cl., 57
Boswell's Court, 9
" Bovril," 94
[Bow Head], 21
[Boyd's Cl.], 90
Brodie's Close, 23
[Brown's Court], 84
Buccleuch Statue, 26
Buchanan's Court, 24
Bull's Cl., 98
Burnet's Cl., 60
Byers Cl., 34

C

Callender's Entry, 84
Calton Road, 88
Campbell's Cl., 83

Cannon Ball House, 4
Canongate Church, 78
    do.   Churchyard, 79
    do.   Tolbooth, 77
    do.   No. 184, 94
Cant's Cl., 65
[Cap and Feather Cl.], 45
Carrubbers Cl., 46
Castle, 1
Castle Hill Walk, 3
Castle Wynd, 8
Chalmers Cl., 50
Chancellor's Court, 100
Chessels Court, 90
Clam Shell House, 60
[Coalstoun's Cl.], 10
Cockburn Street, 45
Cockpen House, 6
[Coull's Cl.], 73
Covenant Cl., 59
[Craig's Cl.], 39
Cranston Street, 73

D

[Dickson's Cl.], 65
[Donaldson's Cl.], 19
Dunbar's Cl., Canongate, 81
[do.   ], Lawnmarket, 19

F

Fisher's Cl., 23
Fleshmarket Cl., 44
Fountain Cl., 70

G

[Galloway's Cl.], 18
Geddes Entry, 41
Gentles Cl., 97

4